WHY CHOOSE HELL WHEN YOU CAN HAVE HEAVEN ON EARTH?

A Guide To Sustaining A Positive Attitude In A Troubled World

Dr. Joseph Lathan

ISBN: 1539154866
ISBN 13: 9781539154860

DEDICATION

This book is dedicated to those seeking comfort from the loss of loved ones and to those who desire to live life to the fullest on Earth.

ACKNOWLEDGEMENTS

I want to first and foremost thank my "Higher Power" entity in which I refer to as The God of Israel. Special acknowledgement to my beautiful wife Pamela for her love and support since our union 18 years ago. To my three wonderful daughters and my three beautiful granddaughters who fill my heart with joy. I also like to thank my awesome family and dear friends who have always stood by my side and believed in me to do great things. I would be remised if I fail to acknowledge my spiritual mentor, Bishop Allen Cox and the teachings of The Spiritual Israel Church and Its Army for the acquisition of wisdom, knowledge and understanding of life. Lastly I would like to thank my dear friend and colleague, Dr. Concetta Gallo for her copyediting assistance to make this book a quality product for readers to enjoy.

CONTENTS

INTRODUCTION

As a minister and church pastor, the majority of people I know and meet carry a worldview that we have to die to go to Heaven and hopefully live worthy enough in the eyesight of God to avoid a trip in the opposite direction to that place called "Hell." While this philosophy may permeate our society, I have always had an issue with accepting such a belief. I always felt it was pointless for God to make His most precious work, after His own image and likeness (Genesis 1:27), live a temporal, unfulfilled life. I questioned why we have to die to reach Heaven or Hell when He created us to be joyful and prosperous human beings to live on Earth.

This book is intended to open a dialogue on God's plan for mankind at the beginning of creation and how we can enjoy life to the fullest despite the tragedies we see in the paper, on the news or in our own personal experiences. Some may question how to find joy in a world full of violence, but let this book be a guide to sustain a positive attitude in a troubled world by understanding God's master plan. Based on multiple references from the Holy Bible, and the adoption of a mindset that desires to see beauty in an ugly world, my prayer is that you will become empowered to experience Heaven on Earth. This book will share the secrets of God's master plan from the beginning of creation and dispute a world philosophy that it's impossible to be joyful on a daily basis.

While some may believe that joy and happiness are synonymous, one of the first secrets that I will share is the difference between the two. I like to view happiness as a positive emotion, yet as one that is dependent upon things that happen and is more external in nature. If things happen to work in one's favor, than the level of happiness increases. But if the same individual falls victim to negative experiences, then the level of happiness greatly decreases based on, again, what happens. Joy is as a state of being and more internal in nature. Joy is not dependent on external stimuli, as its strength resides in faith in a higher being or a power bigger than oneself. In the face of trouble, happiness is MIA (missing in action), but should trouble enter into joy's territory, joy manages to sustain a level of hope despite the absence of a smile.

This book will not debate or promote any one religious view; it has the intention to service a broad, pluralistic audience. I am keenly aware that people of different faiths or ethnic groups may refer to God or a higher power by many different names. While I may refer to my own personal higher power entity as The God of Israel, others may choose to use other familiar names as God, Jesus, Allah, Jehovah and a host of other names. In an effort to unify a core belief amongst all those who may read this book, I will use God and other ecumenical terms such as "Creator of Life" to reference the highest power of existence on the positive level and "Ruler of Darkness" for what some call, Satan, Lucifer or the Devil to reference the extreme negative level of existence.

This book will incorporate personal stories and life experiences that convey my own challenges to inspire others that life is what you make it despite the potential for failures and setbacks. These eyes have seen many things in my 46 years of existence, and life has been no cakewalk. People may see the smile on my face and joy in my heart displayed on a daily basis, but most have no idea how I got there. Like many of you now reading this book, I have not been exempt from trials and tribulations. I've had my share of alcohol and drug use, and I know what being laid off and fired from a job feels like. I have been married more than once, had children at a young age and know the grave pain a divorce can cause. I experienced the hardships of single parenting and what paying child support feels like. I've experienced financial ruin to the point where I had to file for bankruptcy and cannot forget what it feels like to leave my family, loved ones and friends to relocate to a different state for a new start on life. Ultimately, I sat on the front pew at a funeral with three caskets lined in the front to mourn the loss of family patriarchs that were instantly killed in a car crash in the act of doing a good deed.

These are just some of the things in my personal life that I share to encourage others. I don't feel sorry for myself or regret my past experiences, as they have refined me into who I am today. Despite all that I've been through, I found comfort and hope in the Creator of Life to become a recent PhD graduate, co-pastor of a church in Harlem, NY, a senior college administrator for one of the largest community colleges in the U.S., a new business owner, a published author, a devoted husband, a faithful father and a friend to anyone in need. I have felt some of life's greatest joys and deepest sorrows, yet through my hardships, I decided long ago to not let my circumstances determine my attitude about life. This positive perspective simply comes from me choosing to see more joy than pain.

CHAPTER 1

FROM STICKS TO BRICKS

I t's the year 2016, and who would have thought, more than 18 years ago, a country boy who grew up on a farm would be living in Brooklyn, New York. As a teenager, I remember the impact and influence that New York artists, such as KRS-1, Dana Dane, Slick Rick, Biggie Smalls, P-Diddy and so many others had on my life. The songs often mentioned landmarks and streets like the Boogie-Down Bronx, Delancey Street, Queensbridge, Do or Die Bedstuy and a number of other places that were foreign to me growing up. I can never forget the impact New York movies like *Do The Right Thing, New Jack City* and *Jungle Fever* made in my life. As a spectator enjoying the movies, I had no clue that I would actually be living in New York and experience the sites in person.

As I reflect on my amazing journey, it's hard to believe that I managed to adjust to a city with more than eight million people coming from my humble beginnings in the country raised on a farm. To go to work and other places around the city, I ride the subways like millions of other New Yorkers on a daily basis. I enjoy the quietness and nature sounds of the country, and it's hard to believe that I'm now used to the constant sounds of car horns and police sirens. New York traffic can be like no other, but now the traffic has become part of my norm, and I have no problem driving in a city that's not so driver friendly, to say the least. How did I get here? Let's take a few steps back and I will share a brief historical background of how I went from sticks to bricks.

NO ORDINARY BIRTH

In 1969, a child was born to James H. and Ruthie Mae Lathan: their last of 10 children on a late December afternoon. It was also the same day Ruthie (my mother) almost lost her life during the delivery. I can recall her telling me the story of the out-of-body experience she felt during my birth.

> "After birthing nine children, I couldn't believe the level of pain I felt when having you. I was so tired and weak that I just wanted to give up and go to sleep. I closed my eyes and felt my spirit leaving my body, and there was no more pain. The doctor was calling my name and slapped me, and I awoke at the same time delivering you."

She then proceeded to share what the doctor said after the near-death experience,

> "Mrs. Lathan, I have delivered all 10 of your children, and after this experience, should you ever conceive again, find another doctor because I almost lost you."

That was my arrival into the world. You could say my mother and I were experiencing the breath of life at the same time. It was my first, and she fought so that it wouldn't be her last. My life has never been easy, and it was evident at birth. That experience set the tone for the first of many challenges to come.

I grew up in a rural area, about 50 miles outside the city of Detroit, Michigan, in a place called Maybee. Yes, that's correct:

Maybee spelled with two "e"s. The joke that I often hear when I share with others where I'm from is, "Maybe Maybee is a real place, maybe it is not!" It was a very small town, with a population of less than 500 people who were predominately Caucasian, and the majority of the African-American population lived outside of the small town mainly on one street named Tuttle Hill Road.

We lived in the country with every domestic animal imaginable on a farmland. My father, James, was known as a man of many talents and even built the two-bedroom home that we lived in, which was surrounded by 5 ½ acres. You can imagine the closeness we shared as a family when all the children still lived at home. The first of the siblings passed in her infancy, but at one point there were 11 people (nine children and two adult parents) living in a two-bedroom home with one bathroom. Most of the acres on our land were used for planting and harvesting crops for selling at the weekly farmers market. The rest of the crops we raised were used to feed the family. Having many children is very important when you live on a farm because the more hands a family has, the more help it has.

MR MCGEE

As the youngest of 10 children, responsibilities came very early in life. While I was a part of the family workforce as early as 7 years old, I landed my first real job at the tender age of 10. My boss' name was Mr. McGee, a retired automotive worker. After retirement, he took up farming and became very successful at it, owning more than 100 acres of land in the next town over, called Milan. Having so much land and so many crops to manage, my family was often hired by Mr. McGee during the summer to pick bushels of peas, crates of greens, corn, squash, watermelons and a plethora of other crops to sell at the local farmers market.

As a child, I loved to play and have fun just as much as the next child did but always jumped at the chance to make some money.

3

Often, I would volunteer to help my mother and father around the house and provide some meaningful help despite being so young. When I turned 10 years old, Mr. McGee wanted me to continue working for him during the school year after the summer was over. Every day after school, when I got off the school bus, Mr. McGee would be there waiting in his white car to take me to his land to work.

People were quite amazed when they saw a 10-year-old boy driving a tractor and farming at such a young age. I missed out on many activities with the neighborhood children; while they were having fun, I was being responsible and working. I wanted to work so I could make my own money without depending solely on my parents, and my hard work really paid off when Mr. McGee brought me my first brand-new bike.

I felt a strong sense of accomplishment when I rode down the street on my shiny new chrome dirt bike. All my friends pleaded to ride, but I was not quick to comply to their request. I felt that they didn't sacrifice like I did to earn the privilege to ride my new wheels. Having a brand-new bike while all my friends had used bikes was the first confirmation for me that if you work hard, good things happen. That experience set the tone for my work ethic, which followed me into my adult years. Hard work really does pay off.

One day, around the age of 13, I came home from school and Mr. McGee's car was not in the driveway. I went inside to get dressed as usual and waited for his arrival, but he never showed. As I was waiting on the front porch, my dad's car pulled in the driveway about 15 minutes later. With a fifth of Jack Daniels in his hand, Dad summoned me over to the car and said, "Your boss man is dead! He had a heart attack behind the wheel on his way to pick you up and hit a truck head on and he died instantly." I was in shock! My mouth went numb, my throat got tight, and tears filled my eyes and rolled down my cheeks.

Although I was very sad and wished Mr. McGee had not died, I realized I could have been in the car and lost my life too. That was the day that I formed a special bond with the Creator, and I began to believe that I was made for a special purpose. I was still young and didn't know what that purpose might be, but I had always noticed that I was different from the other children I grew up with, even my own siblings.

My childhood experience and growing up on a farm helped me to establish a strong foundation that prepared me for what was to come. Throughout my childhood and teenage years, it was as though I lived under attack by the Ruler of Darkness. I constantly got hurt, sick or in trouble with the law, and my mother prayed continuously for my safety. Despite all the attacks, I now see that there were angels encamped all around me that protected and guided me through each trial and tribulation. As I entered into young adulthood, I understood and accepted that I was not an ordinary person but was designed for a special purpose. I was still seeking what that purpose might be.

14 YEARS OLD AND FATHERLESS

It was Memorial Day, 1984, when my mother and older sisters returned home from the hospital to tell us the bad news. We knew that Dad was in the hospital and that they went to visit him but never expected to hear that he would not be coming home. In my mind, he was like Superman, and I thought nothing could defeat him! My father always hated the hospital, but Mom finally convinced him to go. What he had feared most was confirmed. He was sick, and the diagnosis was cancer! The Jack Daniels he drank straight from the bottle was his treatment for the pain that he felt. He was old-school, and his generation was not too big on letting their family know when they got sick, especially the children. If he hated hospitals, then you can imagine he didn't want the doctors cutting on him. But by the

5

time he sought treatment, the cancer was already in an aggressive stage, so surgery sounded like the best option to take. Days after the operation, he died.

Although my father passed when I was very young, I'm grateful to have known my father and learned so much from him in the short amount of time that we had together. I was his Baby Boy and held a special place in his heart because I often asked him if he needed my help. Helping him around the farm was the way I spent quality time with him, and he was eager to teach me everything he knew. It was hard to believe that I was without a father at such a young age, and I was somewhat jealous of the neighborhood kids who still had their fathers in their lives.

MOVE TO THE CITY (MONROE)

I was in 8th grade when my father passed. After his funeral services and final farewell, Mom decided it was time to leave the country life. While Mom dealt with the country life for many years, in all actuality, she was a city girl at heart. She felt the country was no longer the place for us with the absence of Dad, since he was the one that kept everything on the land in order. Most of the older siblings had moved out on their own, so Mom knew that staying on the land was not the best option. Ruthie decided it was time to leave the country, and we moved to the city of Monroe.

Monroe is approximately 20 miles south of Maybee, and although not far away from where I grew up, it was considered a major city in my mind. When you lived in a town with a population of less than 500 people and moved to a place where there were over 130,000 people, you can imagine the difference of the two lifestyles. I was becoming acclimated to my newfound environment, and I no longer had to work in the fields to manage the crops or feed the animals. Ruthie searched the daily paper and located a home for rent on Kentucky Avenue. There was only three siblings left to finish school, and we were now residents of Monroe.

Monroe was famous for giving people nicknames, and everyone seemed to have one. Whether you liked the nickname or not, people gave you one, and once the name got out, everyone called you by your newly adopted name. You can imagine the first nickname I inherited after our move. They referred to me as "Country Boy." I didn't care for the name, but I was the new kid and didn't make a fuss to try to fit in.

I was not a total stranger to my new environment, as the majority of my older siblings lived in Monroe, and I had made some friends prior to the move. Ninth grade was when I began attending school in Monroe, and I was a very good athlete. I was one of the starting running backs on the football team and made the starting line up on the basketball team. Along with my athletic ability, I was a good student and maintained a 3.8+ GPA during my entire junior high and high school years.

Being a good athlete and student, I began to develop a core group of friends who had the same priorities that I had. We were a special group of student athletes and took pride in achieving at a high level. We were just like any other teenagers growing up who loved to have fun, go to parties and do all the other things that teenagers that age do. But my core group of friends and I believed in staying out of trouble, doing well in our academics and making money. We kept each other straight and were not afraid to speak up when one of us were heading in the wrong direction, or would do something really stupid.

Today, we still encourage each other, and I'm grateful to have found true friends who are still close after being out of high school for nearly 30 years and are over 700 miles away. As good friends do, we still will let each other know when one of us makes a bad move or does something stupid, even in our adult life. That's just what good friends do!

HIGH SCHOOL SWEETHEART

Despite being an academic scholar and athlete, I had no desire to go out of state to attend college. The following year, I graduated from high school and attended a local college so that I could stay close to home, my family, my church and my high school girlfriend, who I married four years later. Of all the girls in Monroe, she was the girl that I had to have, so I thought. We were friends when we met in ninth grade, and she was from a family that was rather wealthy compared to my humble beginnings and family financial status.

She and her family lived on what was known as the rich side of town, where hardly any Black people lived. I would periodically go by her house to visit as friends; her mother thought I was a really nice guy. I was going out with other girls while in school but always had my sight set on my high school sweetheart. Whenever I would see her in school, I would try to strike up a conversation to see if one day she might be interested in going out with me. I knew it was a long shot because she was one of the most popular girls in school and I was a "country boy" with a wardrobe that one could say was less than stylish.

It was 11th grade, and school had started, but I noticed that my high school crush didn't show up for the start of the school year. She had been gone all summer, and I later learned that she was pregnant by an older guy from out-of-state. When she returned back to Monroe towards the end of the 11th grade school year, she returned with a baby girl. She and the baby's father were not together, and she returned back to Monroe High to complete the remainder of school until graduation.

I learned that when a man thinks he found that special one, he will do and overlook many things to be with the person he wants. Now that she was back in town, I decided this was my chance, despite her having a child. We rekindled our friendship, and I would periodically go over her house to visit, as both of our families now stayed in the same apartment complex since her return.

Then it happened! One summer, my best friend and I decided to double date, and I asked my high school sweetheart if she would go out with me, just as friends. She accepted, and her mother thought it was nice that we were going out, as long as we were just friends. I was raised to be courteous and a gentleman and having five sisters taught me how to treat a lady, which is what her mother said she liked in a young man.

That was the night we had our first kiss, and I felt like I was floating on cloud nine. She was the person that I dreamed about dating, and like they say, "Be careful what you ask for because you just might get it." We were from two different worlds, but that didn't matter to me. By the beginning of our senior year, we were officially dating, and I was fully acclimated to my new environment and accepted by my peers as "one of them." They no longer called me Country Boy; I had adopted a much cooler nickname, and life was good. I was well liked by teachers and school administrators, I was captain of the basketball team and I had the girl of my dreams. I felt like I was on top of the world and life couldn't get better. Boy was I so wrong!

HIGH SCHOOL SWEETHEART GONE SOUR

During our senior school year, my relationship with my high school sweetheart was like a see-saw in perpetual motion. We constantly broke up and got back together time and time again. After we graduated, we still tried to make a go at our relationship, but it was evident that we were two different people. When you are blinded by so-called love, it's amazing how everyone can see things about your relationship that you somehow miss. My family, especially my mother and oldest sister, knew that we were on different pages and would advise me to let the relationship go for both of our sakes. To make matters worse, her mother felt the same way about me. Her mother did not feel the same way about me as her daughter's boyfriend as she felt about me as her daughter's friend. They knew we were a mismatch, but we were determined to prove them wrong. So we thought!

Life after high school was a nightmare and one of the most confusing times of my life. My high school sweetheart and I went to local colleges so that we could still date. Just like high school, we would make up and break up and somehow found a way to get back together and eventually marry. During the early part of our marriage, we had two more girls to add to the one that I accepted as my own when she was only a few years old. I wanted so badly to make our marriage work for the sake of our three children, but that never happened.

Life as a young married couple with children was hard. I was working two jobs and hustling on the side to make ends meet after I dropped out of college in my sophomore year. No matter how hard I worked, it seems like we could never get ahead. We often argued and disagreed on a regular basis, and as we got older, we realized that we were two different people on different paths. I finally caught a break in 1995 and was hired at Ford Motor Company, which provided more financial stability for my family, but my ex-wife and I had come to the conclusion that we were better apart. After 10 years of trying to work things out, I had to accept the reality about my marriage: there was none.

I had been so mentally battered and bruised from the stress of our marriage that I metamorphosed into a total different character than others knew me to be. I had lost my upbeat, optimistic spirit, and my kind disposition turned rather cold and distant. Even I didn't know the person I saw when I looked in the mirror. As the home environment was in constant disarray, I moved out of our home, leaving everything but my clothes, and found a house in Milan that rented rooms.

After months of solitude, it was in my one room living quarters that I found myself once again. Although the room was small, I found a sense of peace to help realign myself with my character. I was the chairman of the deacon's board at my local church and immersed myself in church activities as a means of running from my hurt past. I despised the fact that I was in a failed relationship and filled the void by trying to spend as much time as I could with my daughters in my small room, which had a park a few steps away. They didn't care that it wasn't the big house with lots of yard space to play in. The girls were just happy to spend some quality time together with their father playing simple games or playing in the park. As young ladies now in their 20s, we still reminisce about the time we often played tag on the jungle gym. The girls loved the challenge of trying to catch me as I maneuvered the jungle gym, which was one of our favorite games at the time. Those were the times we formed a special bond that would become instrumental a few years later when I revealed that I was moving to New York

A VISIT TO THE EAST COAST

Ten years after my high school graduation, I had a chance to travel to New York City for the first time with my big sister Janie to attend a weekly church conference. I was still living in my small room, working at Ford Motor Company. I continued to serve as the chairmen of the deacon board at my local church and felt honored to hold the position, being the youngest deacon in the church at that time. Engulfed in my work and church responsibilities and spending as much time as I could with my girls, my big sister knew that I could use a much-needed vacation.

She was traveling to New York with her children and invited me and my two youngest daughters to join her. I felt it was exactly what I needed to help break the monotony of my life. The relationship between my ex-wife and I was officially over, and after years of separation, I filed for divorce. We both agreed that it was time to move on with our lives, realizing that we were very young when we began our relationship and that people change.

Being in New York for the first time was amazing and intimidating at the same time! I had never seen so many people in one area at one time other than a major sporting event or concert. The drivers were very aggressive and the sound of beeping horns was constant. There were so many lights and billboards, and I understood why they called it the city that never sleeps. It was springtime, and I had never seen tulips so tall in such an assortment of colors. Who could forget the shopping and tasting so many different ethnic foods? I was in New York experiencing a side of city life that I only could imagine being a country boy! Most people who visit New York quickly admit that it's a nice place to visit but not a place to live. Ironically, I thought the same thing on my first visit, and who would have thought less than a year later I would be a resident of Brooklyn.

A NEW START AT LOVE

When I returned from New York, I felt different. Coming from my humble Maybee roots, I was exposed to a side of life so much bigger than what I was accustomed to. I accepted the fact that I would soon be divorced and assumed my routine of work, church and parenting, but something was missing. I had begun to pick up the pieces of my life but felt the need for companionship. Yes, there were a few girls after my separation that I tried to date that didn't materialize into lasting relationships because I was hesitant to begin a new one. I can now see that I was not mentally healthy for a new relationship because I still carried so much baggage from my previous one. Metaphorically speaking, having too many bags in one room can make it hard for two people to stay in the same room.

I was a wounded bachelor trying to make his way back onto the court but failed to make the winning shot in the dating game. But despite my reservations, I wanted to take a chance on that special someone and tried to go to places where I could possibly meet the woman of my dreams. I became frustrated and wondered why it was so hard for me to find someone that I could begin a meaningful relationship with because, in my eyesight, I thought I was a good catch.

I now realize that although I thought I was a good catch, I had a wounded aura that other people (successful women) could see or feel. I was internally damaged, and although I may have dressed well, my spiritual aura revealed the true character behind the clothes to those who were spiritually inclined. It's almost like a bad smell that everyone else can smell on you but you. It was improbable to find a quality relationship if I couldn't change my aura, and I began to pray to the Creator to create in me a clean heart and renew a right spirit in me (Psalms 51:10).

I wanted to be relieved of my bitter, hurtful past and began to pray for God to send me my Eve, just as He brought Adam his wife (Genesis 2:22). I had dedicated so much of my time to working and participating in church activities that I believed He would give me the desire of my heart from my devotion to Him. I began to wonder if God really was listening to me. Despite my dedication and busy schedule, I still felt lonely and longed for that special someone.

WHEN CHANGE CALLS YOUR NAME

Have you ever heard how one person can change your whole life? Well, that's what happened to me, and 18 years later, it is evident that my life has taken a drastic change from the dirt roads and farm land, to the bright lights of the city. It was the summer of 1998 during our annual two-week church conference in Michigan when my Eve showed up. She was from New York, and as a young man growing up in the church, I always noticed and admired her from afar whenever she would come to town.

She was tall and classy with a strong New York accent, but I always felt our age difference, social status and distance apart would never allow me a chance to win her heart. Our families had known each other our entire lives, but I never imagined that we would become a couple. We were from two very different places, and besides, she was six years older than me.

Yes it's true, one person can change your whole life, and after my first visit to New York in April of 1998, I was living in Brooklyn nine months later. It all started the last week of our annual June church conference, and after nearly two weeks of services and church activities, I was ready to go out somewhere to have some fun and let off some steam.

It was Friday night in Detroit when I decided that I would go out after the conference. I was by myself, and when I walked into the doors of a very popular place called Club Yesterdays, I looked across the room and saw some ladies I knew who had also attended the conference that night. The majority of the ladies were from Michigan, but there was one lady with them from New York who I was very attracted to.

I walked across the room to their table and said hello and asked if it was okay to sit down and chat. They agreed, and as we sat and talked about the conference, I particularly had my eye on the one from New York. As the night progressed, the conversation turned into a one-on-one with her and me. I was surprised to learn that she was not in a committed relationship with anyone, which prompted me to put my best foot forward. I felt this would be my one and only chance to strike her interest.

I invited her on the dance floor, and we had a few dances and continued to talk intensely. I became so centered on knowing more about this incredibly beautiful woman that it was almost as though the girls she came with didn't exist. The conversation was going so well, and it was hard to believe that she also wanted to know more about me. The closing time for the club was fast approaching and I didn't want the night to end. She was staying close to where I lived outside of the city, so I asked if I could treat her to an early morning breakfast at a 24-hour diner along the way. I was thrilled she agreed, and we said our goodbyes to the other ladies as she jumped in her car and followed me in my car towards our destination.

After arriving to the diner and ordering some food, we talked into the wee hours of the morning. I didn't want the date to ever end, but the daylight confirmed that we had been up all night and probably needed to sleep. As we jumped into our cars and parted ways, I felt like the luckiest man in the world. She was attracted to me just as much as I was attracted to her, and we decided that we would stay in contact regularly. We enjoyed each other's company and had so much in common that it made me wonder if this could really be happening to me. When I saw her the following day, inside my heart fluttered uncontrollably, but outside I wanted to appear as though I was cool, calm and confident. She was not only smart and beautiful but also a successful career woman and I couldn't believe she was single. She had my full attention!

The conference ended a few days later and everyone was leaving to return to their home states. We were aware the distance between us would be a challenge for a relationship, but we exchanged contact information so that we could at least stay in touch. After her return to New York, we spoke often on the phone or via email. I felt like things were heading in the right direction to consider a more serious relationship until a few months later: the return phone calls and emails slowed down and eventually stopped. I was puzzled! I didn't know why she chose to communicate less frequently but had an idea that it might be someone else in the picture.

The very next conversation we had, I felt the need to know why the sudden change in communication and boldly asked if there was someone else that she was seeing. She then explained to me that she had been periodically seeing someone before we met and that they had decided that they would make an attempt as a couple. She was very apologetic when she broke the news, and since we were not officially dating, I had to respect her decision.

Although extremely disappointed to hear such news, I felt a strong bond and desired the opportunity to perhaps take our relationship to the next level, and I was convinced that our meeting back in Detroit was fate. She was surprised that I took the news so well and even more surprised when I responded for her to feel free to move forward with her current relationship but that she would one day be with me. I told her that I would wait for her because I was convinced that she was my Eve and I was her Adam. Knowing that she was involved with someone else, I respected her relationship and didn't want to interfere with any more phone calls or emails unless she wanted to talk.

A few weeks later, my phone rang and it was her. We began periodic communication once again, and a few after that she then revealed that the guy she was seeing was no longer in the picture. When she delivered the news over the phone, inside my heart raced with excitement but I felt the need to play it cool. I then reminded her that I was serious about waiting for her, and now that the guy was out of the picture, I made it clear that I was still very interested in her. Once again we began speaking on a daily basis, and I felt it was time to pay a visit to New York just to see how far our relationship would take us.

Having a sister-church in New York, we agreed that I would come and visit during their annual October event. We were both very attracted to each other but didn't know how far the relationship would go, being nearly 700 miles apart. During those couple of days, we learned so much more about each other, and I knew then that she was the one for me. She made it known that she liked me but was not sure she could do any more long-distance relationships. After my return back to Michigan, I understood the challenge of a long-distance relationship. We decided to try to take it slow, but the speed of the relationship only increased as we continued to talk daily over the phone. I was starting to fall in love.

In December of 1998, I returned to New York to celebrate the New Year with her, and we made it official that we would date each other exclusively. The fact that she promised not to get involved in any more long-distance relationships and that she would not date anyone younger than her signaled that she really did like me. By the end of the trip, we were assured that we would make a good couple, and leaving to return home to Michigan was very disheartening for both of us. We were in love and we knew it!

Upon my return home, the phone calls and emails got more intimate and intense. It was hard to believe that I had found love but that it was miles away. I discovered that when you find true love, it is extremely hard for two people to maintain a meaningful relationship with someone else in another state, so something had to change. The periodic visits and phone calls no longer sufficed.

The thought of me moving came to mind, but I couldn't fathom surviving without the income of Ford Motor Company, nor how I would survive without seeing my daughters on a regular basis. Additionally, as the chairman of my local church, with much responsibility, I wondered who would do my job if I moved. It felt like it would be too drastic of a change for everyone. The following months were worse as I fell deeper in love but still felt torn due to my sense of loyalty to my life in Michigan

Despite the many responsibilities I had, being exposed to New York living made my life in Michigan much less appealing. I was making at least $75,000 a year without overtime or a college degree and knew it would be hard to find something comparable elsewhere. Most important, my two youngest daughters were still very young, and I knew they would miss me as much as I would miss them if I moved. Then I thought about the pain I had experienced over the last decade in my previous relationship and how my new relationship seemed to form out of nowhere. Our union and how we met seemed divine. We were not looking for each other but found each other, so I proposed that I would move in March of 1999 if she agreed to take the relationship to the next level.

She asked if I was certain that moving was what I really wanted to do. I was convinced that the Creator had put us together by the magical way we met, and I assured her it was what I wanted to do despite all the unknowns I was yet to face. One week prior to my departure, I told Ford Motor Co. that I was resigning. After being there for five years, I signed my resignation papers to confirm that I voluntarily quit. I was operating on pure faith and I didn't have a job waiting for me in New York and not sure how the temp agencies appointments would go once I got there. I broke the news to my family, and the majority was happy for me after seeing what I had been through in my previous marriage. Other members were both happy and sad because they knew my regular presence would be missing.

Breaking the news to my two youngest daughters was hard. They were old enough to understand that I was moving but still young enough to not really comprehend that they would not see me on a regular basis. When my ex-wife found out that I was moving, she became very angry and vowed that I would not speak or see them if I moved. I love my girls, but I was dying inside and had outgrown living in Michigan. Leaving Michigan was one of the hardest decisions I had ever made in my life, but I knew I had to. I felt a calling to my life on the East Coast, and the new love of my life was the catalyst for the move, but there was so much more that God had in store for me. 18 years later, it is evident that the move was in fact the right move for me.

It was Saturday March 20th, the day I moved. The day before I left, I packed my little red Toyota Tercel with my clothes and other belongings and was planning the drive to New York. Ironically, there had been a snow storm during the night, and I woke up to

8-10" of snow on the ground. My present wife, then girlfriend, asked if I was sure it was a good idea to leave with the weather being like it was. I was determined to stick to the plan because I felt if I didn't leave according to my plan, I might not follow through with it.

Due to the snow-covered roads, there were both cars and trucks that had slid off the road along the way, but my small car managed to trudge through the snow and stay on the road as I traveled east. Saturday night around 9 pm, I pulled up to my new home in Brooklyn.

CHAPTER 1 SUMMARY:

Chapter 1 presented a brief summary of my life story, from being raised on a farm in the country to one day becoming a PhD, college administrator and pastor of a church in the big city of New York 18 years later. The road that I now travel was filled with many speed bumps, potholes and detours, but I managed to continue to forge ahead despite the many obstacles and setbacks. During that time, I shed many tears and felt lost and confused on a number of occasions, but I continued to put my faith in a higher power for direction and hope.

There were times that I questioned if New York was the place for me or if I should move back home to my original comfort zone with all my family and friends. I knew life back home would not be as challenging as living in NYC, and I often had to remind myself that my arrival in New York was by no accident. Over the last 18 years living in NYC, I have seen and learned many life lessons, and today I have a full understanding of what my purpose for moving to the East Coast was. I always believed and now can attest to the fact that it's not where you are from but where you are that matters most, and I have learned to survive and excel in both country and city environments. Many of the learned lessons came through trial and error, but over the years I managed to pick up the pieces, learn from my mistakes and put myself in a position to excel in life.

Now that I have shared the many twists and turns of my life story, the remainder of this book will share biblical and spiritual truths learned along the way. I can now reflect on how I succeeded to become the leader that I am today despite all the personal challenges I have faced in my lifetime. Through faith in the Creator of Life and a belief that I was created for a divine purpose, I sought to understand the overall purpose of humankind. My research has led me to the beginning of our world as we know it from the story of creation as told in the Holy Bible, which can be seen as the blueprint of God's master plan for mankind.

Chapter 2 will explore the story of Adam and Eve to recapture what God's master plan is and unfolds His purpose for His greatest creation: man and woman. Unlike the disobedient act of Adam and Eve, this chapter will also explore the life of Moses and his challenges to provide insight into the miraculous power available to us through our obedience and trust in the Creator. Often our trials and tribulations are great teaching points if we can persevere and learn from them. The shared teaching points in the following chapter will help you discover and maintain a heavenly position right here on Earth by understanding God's plans at the beginning of time.

CHAPTER 2
GOD'S MASTER PLAN

I magine life with minimal challenges, healthy, happy and free in an eternal state of bliss. This was actually God's master plan for humankind in the beginning. Most of us have heard the Bible story of Adam and Eve and the Garden of Eden. This particular place was known as paradise and a place where the couple were to live happy and care free. The term "paradise" represents our Creator's desire for us to enjoy the best that life has to offer, and worry, sickness and death were not in the plan at the beginning of creation. Life was simple! According to the Bible story, Adam and Eve failed to follow God's plan, and their disobedience and bad choice prohibited them from enjoying paradise on Earth.

This book will not focus on the Original Sin Theory, which carries a world-view that every man is born a sinner, nor will this book debate the actual existence of the serpent (Satan) or fruit (apple) which they supposedly ate. I have no interest in proselytization or converting others to share the same religious views as mine and will not focus on the theology of the story. Rather, this book examines God's intended purpose for mankind from the beginning of time and how we can recapture the promises made by the Creator of Life in today's time.

Today, people fail to consider the intended purpose of God's ultimate plan at the beginning of creation, and experiencing an everyday supply of joy is a philosophy that most people you come in contact with fail to accept. The acceptance as temporal beings living in a chaotic and ever-challenging world and dying seems like a natural pattern of life based on the results of our daily experiences. However, the beginning of humankind with Adam and Eve in the Garden of Paradise shares a roadmap that illustrates we were made as God's masterpiece and surrounded by everything we needed to be joyous and prosperous. Being made in God's image and likeness (Genesis 1:27), we were made with the purpose of glorifying the Creator through our obedience and good choices so that we might enjoy the best God has to offer while we are alive.

I am a realist and don't dispute that we will have some challenging days. Worry and stress doesn't discriminate against anyone. Yet, through careful examination of God's Master Plan at the beginning, it is clear that His purpose for our lives didn't involve many of the stressors that we experience today. Knowledge is power and having insight of the master plan provides the means for us to realign ourselves with God's intended purpose whenever we feel out of synch with life. The realignment process begins by first realizing that you were made to enjoy life on Earth.

Understanding that sadness and grief was not in the plan, we can then sustain a positive mindset by using the power of our minds to tap into our connection from Heaven (highest vibration of our mind) to Earth (our fleshly body). This is the connection that Jesus spoke of in the Lord's Prayer when he prayed to the Father to "Let thy will be done on Earth as it is in Heaven" (St. Matthew 6:10). This was a holistic request from Jesus to be in an oneness with the Father in mind, body and spirit. The life and writings of Jesus were the example that God used to illustrate how we too can become the sons and daughters of God and enjoy life in Paradise on Earth.

I want to reiterate that despite the financial stress, worries, illness and disease and ultimately death, it is important to know that these challenges were not in the plan of God. Yes, there are some things and circumstances that we have no control over, but keep in mind that our challenges should not divert our attention from the intended purpose for our lives. Just as the Ruler of Darkness used enticing methods to persuade the first man and woman in the Garden of Eden, his plan of attack on our lives has not changed. As a story recorded centuries ago, we have the advantage of reading and examining Adam and Eve's failure to make better choices for our lives.

The story of creation emphasizes the fact that mankind was given a choice. Of course the Creator could have made us operate on instincts like animals or function like the change of the seasons, but humankind was the Creator's most precious work. Along with the power of choice, He also gave Adam dominion over everything on the face of the Earth (Genesis 1:26)

> *And God said, Let us make man in our image, after our likeness: and let them have dominion over the fish of the sea, and over the fowl of the air, and over the cattle, and over all the earth, and over every creeping thing that creepeth upon the earth.*

Having the power of choice and dominion, we are empowered to determine our state of mind, despite the challenges we face. Yes, it may be hard to smile or be joyous when you lose your job, financial security or even a loved one, but the power to choose the negative emotions of grief and sadness still lies with us. It's important to understand that you may not have dominion over your circumstances but you can always have dominion over your reaction to your circumstances.

I may not smile every minute or even every hour of the day, but that does not mean that I'm sad, worried or stressed. Laughing and smiling is not the sole indicator of how much joy one has because joy stems from the inside and is not contingent on the material world. My life is far from perfect, but I'm able to maintain a joyful mindset because of how I choose to view my personal challenges. Seeing challenges as speed bumps and not roadblocks provides hope. Hope is the substance of joy and provides the ability for me to see challenging situations as temporary to avoid being sidetracked by things that happen not always in my favor.

To sustain a high level of joy requires a relationship with a power greater than oneself. As we develop our relationship with the Creator, we then move beyond the physical level (sight, smell, touch, taste and sound) of human, temporal experiences into the realm of the sixth and seventh sense, which is the space where there is a direct connection to a higher power through intuition and discernment. Cultivating our sixth and seventh sense takes practice and when we tap into these levels, we develop hope that operates by faith and not by sight.

Having the insight that your heavenly realm is constantly under attack from both a spiritual and physical level affords one the opportunity to take up arms and go into battle to protect your territory in the form of your peace, joy, love, patience and other fruits of the spirit (Galatians 5:22-23).

WHEN YOU CAN'T MOVE FORWARD, STAND STILL!

From the lack of obedience comes the state of confusion, and when we find ourselves in this state of mind, generally a sense of anxiety and stress are sure to follow. These conditions prevent us from reaching a heavenly mind state. From the story of Adam and Eve, I can envision Eve taking a bite of the forbidden fruit and the perplexed state of mind Adam must have felt as Eve extended her arms for him to partake in the sinful act. It is my assumption that he had to feel very uncomfortable with his decision knowing that God told him what tree to avoid long before Eve was created.

Our obedience to God and following the laws of the land will minimize the state of confusion we experience in our lives on a daily basis. To fight the state of confusion or uncertainty, one of my kingdom thinking philosophies that I practice is this: You don't have to always know what to do, but you should at least know what *not* to do. When you at least know what not to do, you limit the level of confusion you will experience.

It took me a long time to learn that I didn't have to have the answer to every situation or circumstance that life may bring. I didn't have to know what to do at times when I was clueless about life because I felt confident in my relationship with the Creator to guide my next steps. Not knowing what to do at times is a state of mind that happens to many believers of faith; however we should never make poor decisions that make matters worse. The life of Adam and Eve showed us the results making poor choices can cause and making poor choices is an example of what not to do even if you don't know what to do.

When we are in a state of confusion or uncertainty, most often we just need to stand still and hear the voice from within. This point is best illustrated in the book of Exodus when Moses was chosen to lead the Children of Israel from Pharaoh's bondage.

> *And Moses said unto the people, Fear ye not, stand still, and see the salvation of the LORD, which he will shew to you today: for the Egyptians whom ye have seen today, ye shall see them again no more for ever. (Exodus 14:13)*

Despite all the miracles the Children of Israel had seen through the hands of Moses and Aaron, they still had worry and doubt, so Moses took the time to reassure them once again despite what they have already seen the Creator do through the prophet. Moses didn't have all the answers at the time, but when it came time to cross the Red Sea, the Creator told him what to do. With mountains to the left and right of him, Pharaoh's army charging up the rear and a sea of water in front, the Creator from Heaven (within Moses) provided instructions when he needed it most. According to the Bible text, the Creator spoke to Moses, not from the clouds as the movie of the 10 commandments would like to portray, starring Charlton Heston, but rather the Creator spoke to Moses in his mind and spirit. Exodus 14: 15-16 reads:

> *And the LORD said unto Moses, Wherefore criest thou unto me? Speak unto the children of Israel, that they go forward: But lift thou up thy rod, and stretch out thine hand over the sea, and divide it: and the children of Israel shall go on dry ground through the midst of the sea*

It was what we call an "ah hah" moment, and it came when Moses needed it most. We ourselves experience our own personal "ah hah" moments when we feel stuck and an answer seemingly comes to mind. So find peace within yourself at times when you may not know what to do about a certain situation. Understand that these feelings may surface even to those of strong faith, so find the calm through your relationship with the Creator to calm the storm of your ship just as Jesus did for his disciples during their time of storm, as recorded in the Gospel books.

Your state of tranquility in life is often determined by your relationship with the Creator or a Higher Being, and succumbing to worry and stress can result in a blockage or removal from our heavenly state of mind. There are a few points that we can learn from Moses' experience in the book of Exodus to help alleviate the stress and worry that everyday living can bring to diminish our heavenly experience on Earth.

FLAWS AND ALL! GOD IS MORE CONCERNED WITH YOUR FAITHFULNESS THAN YOUR PERFECTION

The Creator is a master at working with people with flaws. He desires that we don't become overburdened with being perfect because that level will only be achieved by Him and through Him. In my lifetime, I'm yet to meet anyone perfect, and according to Mark 10:18, there is no one perfect but the Father.

It is my personal belief that the Creator is interested more in our faithfulness than our perfection because faithfulness means to be dependable and perfection is beyond our reach without Him. When we form a bond with the Creator, the relationship promotes mutual trust that the Creator can depend on us just as much as we depend on Him. I have no problem admitting that I'm not perfect even as a Pastor, yet I feel the Creator's extraordinary power working in me and through me on a daily basis. This power provides the emphasis to achieve a heavenly mind state because of my true friendship with the Creator. I'm not perfect, but I'm faithful and He can depend on me

Moses is a good example of what the Creator can do with what others may consider junk. Although a prominent Bible figure, Moses had his share of flaws. Despite his imperfections, the Creator used him as an example that we too, with our flaws and imperfections, can do great things in our respective area of "calling." In the book of Exodus, Moses felt inadequate or not good enough to lead the Children of Israel from under Pharaoh's bondage due to his inability to speak well. Exodus 4:10 reads:

> *Then Moses told the LORD, "Please, LORD, I'm not eloquent. I never was in the past nor am I now since you spoke to your servant. In fact, I talk too slowly and I have a speech impediment."*

How many times have your inadequacies surfaced in the face of danger? If you lack confidence in yourself, the realm of Heaven can be hard to achieve because the Creator lives in you (St. Luke 17:21), and most often God uses individual people to display His miracle-working power. The more spirit of the Creator you possess, the more confidence you will gain. Not only will you gain more confidence, you also will gain more peace if your mind is stayed on Him (Isaiah 26:3). The confidence gained over time is not confidence in one's abilities or talents alone, but rather it's the confidence gained in the Creator to work on your behalf. This can be described as a heavenly connection—the arrival of the Kingdom on Earth as it is in Heaven.

WHAT'S IN YOUR HAND? SIGNS FROM HEAVEN

I learned that whomever the Creator calls or ordained for special purposes, He also equips for the job. When faced with challenges, often we look out for a solution rather than in. The majority of the time, what we have and whom we know, or what we can do, is sufficient enough for the job. If God is in you (St. Luke 17:21), then what's in you or what you have been equipped with should suffice for any task or challenge (Philippians 4:13). The beginning of Moses' leadership journey found in Exodus Chapter 4: 1-5 is a great example of how he received his first sign from Heaven and a profound passage worth exploring.

And Moses answered and said, But, behold, they will not believe me, nor hearken unto my voice: for they will say, The LORD hath not appeared unto thee. And the LORD said unto him, what is that in thine hand? And he said, A rod. And he said, Cast it on the ground. And he cast it on the ground, and it became a serpent; and Moses fled from before it. And the LORD said unto Moses, Put forth thine hand, and take it by the tail. And he put forth his hand, and caught it, and it became a rod in his hand: That they may believe that the LORD God of their fathers, the God of Abraham, the God of Isaac, and the God of Jacob, hath appeared unto thee.

The story explains how Moses himself felt inadequate, unqualified and lacking the resources to lead the Children of Israel at the beginning of his journey. The Lord needed to prepare Moses for a big job by speaking to his confidence to reassure him that he was the man for the job and that he had all he needed to get the job done. Having an inferior moment, the Creator had to remind Moses what was in his hand.

Moses was so caught up in what he didn't have that he didn't realize that what he had in his hand was sufficient until he was reminded. Moses obeyed the instructions to cast his rod on the ground, and he was startled because it unexpectedly turned into a serpent before his very eyes. To further build his confidence after getting Moses' attention, the Lord instructed Moses to reach out and take the serpent by the tail. Now having more trust in the Creator, Moses obeyed and reached out his hand to grab the serpent by the tail, which then returned back to his rod.

This was not the first time that Moses had to be reminded of what was in his hand. As mentioned at the beginning of this chapter, the same is true when the Israelites fled Egypt and came to the Red Sea with no way of escape in sight. The Creator speaks to Moses once again and asked him that same question when he was preparing Moses for his job in the beginning of the Exodus, "What do you have in your hand?" Being that the Creator had showed him His miracle-working power at the beginning of his mission, Moses had more confidence that what he had in his hand would suffice even though he didn't know what to expect.

The point to be made is that the majority of what we need and the life solutions we seek to overcome our challenges are most often within our reach or in our hands. When caught in a state of uncertainty and feeling inadequate, so often we seek someone for advice and look for help outside of us. Moses discovered that what he needed was already in his hand. If you take the time to stand still to see the salvation of the Lord, you too will discover that you are equipped with everything you need to win. It's nearby! It's in your hand! Let's take a look at Deuteronomy 30: 11-14, which further illustrates how close the answers we seek in life really are:

For this commandment which I command thee this day, it is not hidden from thee, neither is it far off. It is not in heaven, that thou shouldest say, Who shall go up for us to heaven, and bring it unto us, that we may hear it, and do it? Neither is it beyond the sea, that thou shouldest say, Who shall go over the sea for us, and bring it unto us, that we may hear it, and do it? But the word is very nigh unto thee, in thy mouth, and in thy heart, that thou mayest do it.

Take notice of how the last verse of this passage mentions the close proximity of the Word and that it is not far away from us. When you reference St. John 1:1, "In the beginning was the Word, the Word was with God and the Word was God," the scripture assures us how powerful the Word is being a representative of God. The Word we are referring to is not a singular word which describes God in a natural sense. Rather the Word we are referring to is spirit because God is a spirit (St. John 4:24) and also the same word that Jesus had in him based on St. John 1:14: "and the word became flesh and dwelt among us."

Examples of seeking help outside of us include always asking someone else for advice instead of spending quality, meditation time with the Father for Him to reveal the answers you seek. This also applies in money matters when we are looking to borrow money from friends or a bank when you make enough money but fail to spend it wisely.

Ephesian 1:3 reminds us that God has already provided us with all spiritual blessings in heavenly places in Christ. The heavenly place the scripture refers to is in you, and just like the Ragu commercial says, "It's in there!" The Creator has given us everything we need inside of us to overcome or succeed at any challenge. It's in there! If we experience a lack, we have blocked our heavenly connection for the rivers of living water to flow (St. John 7:38). The lack that we experience generally comes from our lack of connection to the Creator of Life.

CHAPTER 3

THE TRUTH
ABOUT HEAVEN AND HELL

As a pastor, Heaven is a regular topic of discussion with others. Most believers that I encounter see Heaven from a physical aspect with the location being way beyond the sun, moon and stars. Additionally, this theology teaches that in order for one to get to this special place, you have to be good and faithful on Earth so that when you die, you can go there. Some ministers really enhance the image of Heaven as a place with pearly gates and streets that are made of pure gold (Revelations 21: 21).

Biblical scholars agree that Revelations is filled with images written by what John saw as futuristic and should not be taken literally. In the book, almost everything John sees is a visual allegory, or a picture to communicate symbolically. If we die and so-called, go up to Heaven, I question how is it possible that our spiritual body would travel to a place way beyond the sun, moon and stars and enjoy the natural images of Heaven with streets of gold, pearly white gates, sweet milk and honey having lost the physical part of who we are. Spirits don't need these types of things to be happy, nor can they eat honey or drink sweet milk.

If we take a moment to use our gifted common sense, one should question the perceptions portrayed of Heaven. The theology that when one dies, we get an opportunity to be reunited with our loved ones who have passed away sounds comforting but not all that believable. I wondered how is it possible to recognize my loved ones who have passed on in Heaven, being that they no longer have a physical body. Our loved ones may lose their physical bodies, but the spiritual body never dies; it has no physical appearance for us to identify specific individuals.

Heaven is perceived as the residence of God, and Galatians 5:22-23 shares the spiritual attributes of God, which consist of love, joy, peace, etc. Being that these attributes are spirit, I believe it will be challenging to identify any one individual in the spirit world. Love, joy and peace are all spiritual attributes that we feel and can only see in the physical body through action. If this is true, how do we recognize our mothers, fathers, sisters or brothers that have passed on in Heaven? In the heavenly world, love is just love and peace is just peace, having no subjection to the physicality of human appearances.

LOCATION IS EVERYTHING

How many times have we heard the business saying, "Location is everything?" Although the saying is very brief, the meaning behind the saying insinuates so much more. On a business level, commercial property that's located in high traffic or readily accessible areas often does more business than businesses where there is less traffic or that are not conveniently located.

Using the business analogy, I thought about the location of Heaven from a spiritual perspective, realizing that my view of its proximity would affect the quality of my heavenly experience. If my perspective of Heaven is ideally located, readily accessible and close to me, I'm afforded more opportunities to experience the direct power of Heaven. This is due to understanding that Heaven is not far from me but at hand.

The average person you meet subscribes to the worldview that Heaven is way beyond the sun, moon and stars, more than 93 million miles away. I often wonder why Heaven has to be way up in the sky and why that philosophy has permeated our society. If we explore the story of creation in the Bible, Genesis 1:8 is the first time Heaven is mentioned and reads:

> *And God said, Let there be a firmament in the midst of the waters, and let it divide the waters from the waters. And God made the firmament, and divided the waters which were under the firmament from the waters which were above the firmament: and it was so. And God called the firmament Heaven.*

If you notice, in Genesis 1:8, God made the firmament and divided the water from the firmament (atmosphere or visible arch of the sky) and God called this particular space Heaven. Under close examination of the aforementioned scripture, you should notice no mention that it's way, way up in the sky or beyond the sun, moon and stars, but this is the location most associate Heaven with.

According to the story of creation, God created Heaven and Earth and separated the waters into bodies of water (seas, lakes, oceans, etc.). On the fifth day of creation, the Bible records that God created the fish to populate the water and the birds to fly above the surface of the Earth, known as "the open firmament of heaven." (Genesis 1:20).

> *And God said, Let the waters bring forth abundantly the moving creature that hath life, and fowl that may fly above the earth in the open firmament of heaven.*

You should know that birds are limited as to how high they can fly into the atmosphere or Heaven. According to science, the highest recorded height of any bird is by whooper swans, which have been seen on radar at a height of 29,000 feet by an airline pilot. While this may be an impressive height, it fails in comparison to the location of the sun, which is said to be 93 million miles away. If the birds fly in the firmament of Heaven, that means that any space above the ground can be considered Heaven, so how did Heaven become a place that was so far away? The Bible does mention three different Heavens in 2 Corinthians 12:2 and this is reason to believe how misinterpretations may have come about. Let's explore the three different dimensions to aid our understanding.

THREE DIMENSIONS OF HEAVEN

From my perspective, based on scripture references, the creation of the firmament of Heaven is the first level and the level that is known as the earth's atmosphere. This provides reason to understand how birds fly in the firmament of Heaven, as mentioned in Genesis. The second level has been described as the outer-space level, which includes the sun, moon and stars. This level of Heaven is also recognized as the natural dimension and one that we can observe with our natural eyes. The third level of Heaven is the spiritual dimension, also known as the residence of God or the Kingdom of God.

Having different dimensions of Heaven can be confusing and gives reason why there are so many different views and interpretations. The purpose of this book is not to dispute others worldviews of Heaven but to provide some insight that may expand our knowledge based on the topic. To be alive and have the ability to enjoy the natural things of life can be described as the first Heaven. This is the level where one can enjoy and experience the physical creation of all things that add to one's quality of life.

The second level can be described as the outer-space area, where the moon and stars exist. The synchronized movement and alignment of the celestial world provides belief that its maker is one of a higher intelligence that cannot be duplicated by humankind. I won't dispute or affirm the Big Bang theory, which some of a more scientific nature subscribe to, but it is my belief that if the celestial world was created by a massive astrological explosion, the Creator of Life was the cause of the explosion. This is referenced in several passages of the Bible, such as mentioned in Isaiah 40: 26 -

Lift your eyes and look to the heavens: Who created all these? He who brings out the starry host one by one, and calls them each by name. Because of his great power and mighty strength, not one of them is missing.

The third level of Heaven is the spiritual dimension and is known as the residence of God, which some refer to as the Kingdom of God. Although God's spirit can exist anywhere, Deuteronomy 10:14 describes the Heaven of heavens as the highest level of Heaven, although all levels were created by God.

Behold, the heaven and the heaven of heavens is the LORD's thy God, the earth also, with all that therein is.

As the spiritual dimension of Heaven, this is the level we reach when we achieve total peace and tranquility within ourselves with the Creator in us. A common worldview held by many is that we have to die to reach this level of Heaven. This philosophy contradicts God's master plan and will for mankind to live and prosper on Earth. I will continue to refer back to God's intended purpose at the beginning and felt it necessary to write this book to share my revelation so that we can learn to experience Heaven while we are alive as opposed to waiting to die and go to it.

Now that we have explored the three different dimensions of Heaven, we can now better discern the natural and spiritual dimensions of each. It is my belief that confusing the two dimensions has caused others to see Heaven as a natural place that we must go to or a place far, far away.

HEAVEN IS AT HAND:

The recorded writings of Jesus giving his disciples instructions to share with the world, explains how close Heaven really is, as referenced in St. Mathew 10:7

And as you go, preach, saying, the kingdom of heaven is at hand.

The passage illustrates the third dimension of Heaven not as a place far, far away but rather a spiritual mindset or an awakening that is attainable and reachable: "at hand." Despite Jesus's reference, many believers subscribe to the philosophy that Heaven is a place that you go to when you die. This is contrary to Jesus's words, as explained in the Lord's Prayer for God's kingdom to come, not die and go to it (St. Matthew 6:10). Based on these scriptural references, Heaven is much closer than you think because it is a spiritual dimension and we ourselves are spirits housed in a natural body. We don't have to die to have a spiritual experience, and if you are prepared to die and go to Heaven, according to Jesus, you will miss the target if Heaven is to come.

So how did the location of Heaven become so far away when the scriptures share that Heaven is at hand and located in you (St. Luke 17:21)?

Neither shall they say, Lo here! or, lo there! for, behold, the kingdom of God is within you.

The reason why we can believe that the kingdom of God in within us is because, according to 1 Corinthians 3:16 -17, we ourselves are the temple of God, not the elements or sky.

> *Know ye not that ye are the temple of God, and that the Spirit of God dwelleth in you?*
> *If any man defile the temple of God, him shall God destroy; for the temple of God is holy, which temple ye are.*

From prior discussion about the three different dimensions of Heaven, the above reference has to be the third Heaven because it explains that it is the residence of God's kingdom. This level supersedes the earthly (first) and atmospheric (second) levels of Heaven referencing that the location is in you.

St. Luke 8:21 should enlighten us even more which reads:

> *And it came to pass afterward, that he went throughout every city and village, preaching and shewing the glad tidings of the kingdom of God: and the twelve were with him,*

Notice how the above passage shares how Jesus not only preached but showed the joy of Heaven to those he came in contact with. The passage never mentions anything about death as a requirement to experience Heaven.

Other misinterpreted references from the Bible can be found in the writings of Paul in his letter to the city of Ephesus, as explained in Ephesians 4:6:

> *One God and Father of all, who is above all, and through all, and in you all.*

Some may read the first part of the scripture (above all) and automatically assume that God is in the sky above. I like to believe that if you continue reading the passage, you will discover that he is not above the sun, moon and stars but rather He is a part of our spiritual being "through us" and "in us." The mention of "above all" should be viewed as the Most High having wisdom, knowledge and understanding that far exceed our human capacity—not "above all" from a natural elevated perspective.

So if Heaven is in you, the next point to ponder is what is it that's in me that makes Heaven, Heaven. The scripture that best answers this question is found in Romans 14:17- 18, which reads:

For the kingdom of God is not meat and drink; but righteousness, and peace, and joy in the Holy Ghost.

Those who believe in God generally don't deny that God's home is Heaven, also referred to as "The Kingdom of God." So the revelation one should receive is that Heaven is not limited to just space above the Earth but also has an internal residence inside every human being. Romans 14:17 reminds us that inner Heaven is not based on the material world (clothes, cars, homes, etc.) but rather it's the internal attributes of God that allow the Heavens to "open up" in our lives.

The above scripture describes righteousness, peace and joy in the Holy Ghost (Spirit of God) as an internal experience as opposed to an external one (meat and drink). Living in harmony with creation and the Creator provides a feeling of completeness and fulfillment of God's intended purpose for humankind on Earth. Entering into this union with the Creator is equivalent to paradise, where negativity or the Ruler of Darkness cannot enter.

You will know if you have reached the heavenly plane by how well you maintain a peaceful, rich state of mind despite daily trials and tribulations. The Ruler of Darkness would like first and foremost that you not enter into this heavenly realm because in that realm we are empowered and he is powerless. I Thessalonians 1:5

clearly reference the power one obtains in the heavenly realm and is represented by actions, not just in words.

For our gospel came not unto you in word only, but also in power, and in the Holy Ghost, and in much assurance; as ye know what manner of men we were among you for your sake.

The power received is not for controlling everything and everyone around you to maintain a positive outlook; rather, the power received is to control one's own actions through alignment with the master plan of God.

Understanding your level of control is important to prevent the feeling of defeat. In our best efforts, we may never be able to control every problem that arrives in our lives on a daily basis, but despite this reality, we still have the power to exercise control over our reaction. A simple parable by one of my favorite ministers said it best: "You can't stop the birds from flying over your head but you can prevent them from building a nest on top of it." Knowing your capabilities and developing the time to spiritually discern things that are in your control and the things that are not provides the power of balance to fully enjoy life on Earth.

Adam and Eve's expulsion from the Garden of Eden was due to their lack of control to align with God's master plan. Although they were given the power of choice, the choices came with consequences that went against the natural order of things.

According to Genesis 3:24, God placed a flaming sword at the entrance of the garden, which prevented Adam and Eve from re-entering the paradise. Like Adam and Eve, we are often kicked out of our heavenly mindset due to our failure to safeguard our heavenly existence. This expulsion often happens through others' words, actions or some unfortunate incident or, in most cases, by our own choices and lack of perseverance. Through understanding and knowing that Heaven is in us and exercising our power of choice, we can utilize the power to remain joyful on Earth despite the many tragedies we hear or read about every day.

Have you ever had a time period in your lifetime, whether it was a month, week, day or even an hour, where everything just seemed to click? Some describe it as "Lady Luck" others as "the flow" and many other names that describe a metaphysical experience. You feel good about yourself knowing your life purpose and pursuing it. These are the moments where death has no sorrow and the things around you have no grave hold over you. Yes, you may hear some sad news or experience some other negative circumstances not in your favor; however, by choosing to remain in Heaven (mentally and spiritually) or maintaining a positive outlook throughout the process you have the opportunity to master this world (your world) and the world to come (your future).

Mastering the Heaven on Earth experience begins with the belief that your Creator is close by and in you. You don't have to pray to a spirit that is millions of miles away but rather can center yourself and speak to the Creator in your spirit and in your heart to enter into oneness. The ability to feel His full vibration and understand His close proximity provides insurmountable strength to overcome any challenge that you may face. I definitely have had my share of life challenges and then some; however, I realize I survived due to the strength drawn from within, having a close neighbor (God) just a door away who I can call in the time of need.

I realize that when you place God in the sky, many, many miles away, you dilute His miracle-working power to operate in your life. Using the analogy of neighbors, ones that live close by have the means to fulfill an immediate need that a neighbor far away cannot. If someone were breaking into my home, clearly the neighbors next door could help guard my home better than ones many doors down.

It's not that the neighbors far away are bad neighbors or not willing to help; they simply live further away and can't possibly see things that take place on my property. Their response to a request or need will generally take more time to fulfill than a good neighbor in close proximity, simply because of the distance. If we realize God's close proximity, we can maximize our peace and our joy to overcome worry, stress and confusion by having a close neighbor to safe guard our property.

THE OPEN WINDOW OF HEAVEN
The book of Malachi provides insight on how we too can have a heavenly experience like the prophet while we are living on Earth. Before the government system of caring for the people, the church was the main care provider. To take care for those less fortunate, people of the city were asked to donate a portion of their goods to the church, which was then distributed as needed. Pay special attention to the last part of the verse and notice how the passage refers to the windows of Heaven being opened by God and the coming of great abundance while Malachi was still living. Malachi 3:10 reads:

> *"Bring the whole tithe into the storehouse, so that there may be food in My house, and test Me now in this," says the LORD of hosts, "if I will not open for you the windows of heaven and pour out for you a blessing until it overflows."*

According to this passage, Malachi didn't have to die to experience Heaven. From being concerned about others and showing true generosity towards all mankind, God promised that he would open the windows of Heaven and pour out blessings that overflow. The opening of Heaven and the pouring of blessings comes in the form of peace, joy, health, happiness, good relationships and many other life-sustaining rewards that Jesus said would come to us: "Thy kingdom come!" as referenced in the Lord's Prayer.

43

Because of the oneness and finished work by God's son, Jesus Christ, "I have finished the work" (St. John 17:4), we now have an example to follow to experience a direct connection to the Creator of Heaven. The above passage clearly confirms that Jesus finished his work, and now it's time we pick up where he left off to finish the work entrusted under our authority.

Matthew 18:18 provides valuable insight on how our heavenly connection operates and reads:

Verily I say unto you, Whatsoever ye shall bind on earth shall be bound in heaven: and whatsoever ye shall loose on earth shall be loosed in heaven.

The passage shares Jesus's teaching of "binding" and "loosing," which is a philosophy that shows the connection to both our spiritual and natural environments to experience a heavenly state of mind on Earth. One way of interpreting this passage is to believe that every natural action and behavior we do reflects the level of our spiritual experiences. When we "bind" or hold on to our peace, joy and happiness at all cost, we can experience the peace of God in our spirit to live freely. When we "loose" or "let go" things that bring discomfort, worry and stress, we eliminate these obstacles from permeating our spiritual being to walk in a oneness with the Creator as Jesus did while he was alive.

Another interpretation of the above passage can be seen as the connection of our human body (Earth) to our mind (spirit). When our mind and our body act in oneness with the Creator of Life, then we are able to do miraculous things and overcome any barrier or challenge we are faced with.

So remember, when you pray, make it a habit to pray to the Creator in your heart and from the highest contemplative state of your mind. This is the Heavenly state! From this practice, you will feel a direct connection to the burden-removing, yolk-binding power of the Creator of Life. This is how you will overcome all things through Christ, which will strengthen you (Philippians 4:13) during your greatest life challenges.

Ultimately, Heaven is a state of mind. Patti LaBelle's hit song, "When You Been Blessed," speaks volumes on the heavenly experience through blessings we receive while on Earth in which we share with others to help rescue them from their Gates of Hell. I can hear Patti now:

When you've been blessed, feel like heaven, heaven
When you've been blessed pass it on, pass it on

Patti's song describes the blessings from God as a heavenly experience while living on Earth. When we have been blessed, the sharing of blessings is part of the requirement to remain in Heaven. The sharing of our blessings can take many forms and include our time, wisdom and knowledge, or our material blessings. Shared blessings provide light for others to also find their heavenly path on Earth. So when you've been blessed, please know that blessings from God are the highest level of blessings from Heaven, and from the many references mentioned above, you should now know that there is no need to die to find Heaven. It's in you!

THE OTHER PLACE: HELL

If the aforementioned is true regarding the location of Heaven being close at hand and in you, one must then ask, where and what is Hell? Have you ever heard someone say, "I'm catching Hell?" The experience they are trying to convey is the emotional state of confusion or pain or the physical experience of sorrow due to some unfortunate or life-altering circumstances beyond their control. Just as Heaven is a state of mind and oneness with the Creator, so

45

is Hell, except there is a oneness with Satan or the negative forces of spiritual wickedness in high places (Ephesians 6:12)

> *For our struggle is not against human opponents, but against rulers, authorities, cosmic powers in the darkness around us, and evil spiritual forces in the heavenly realm (American Standard Version).*

Just as the Creator of Life is a spirit (St. John 3:16), so too is the Ruler of Darkness. The Ruler of Darkness is not a red-colored man with horns and a long tail carrying a pitchfork. Nor is God a white-bearded man sitting way up in the sky surrounded by pearly white gates. These are the images portrayed early in our earthly human existence on television Bible stories or book publications that often carry over into our adult lives. If you question the images of the Creator and the Ruler of Darkness, then you should begin to question the location in which they reside.

THE POWER OF IMAGES

The power of images and words can make a lasting impression on our mentality. When someone mentions the word Satan or the Devil, it's amazing how our mind instantly refers to the image that we have been exposed to growing up. I can never forget the impact the images had on me when I looked at the pictures in the Holy Bible as an impressionable child. I was mesmerized by the colorful images that portrayed a different world than my own. If the Ruler of Darkness is not a red character with horns and a sharp, long tail, then it is safe to assume that he doesn't live in the ground.

As a spirit being, I find it hard to believe that the Ruler of Darkness resides in a physical place underground. There are a number of photos that have been captured by geologists that show what actually does exist at the center of the earth's core. According to scientists, the inner core of the Earth is approximately three thousand miles from the earth's surface with temperatures reaching as high as 11,000 degrees Fahrenheit. We can all agree that the sun can be very hot, but surprisingly, the temperature of the Earth's core is much hotter. While the earth's core may be hot and Hell is depicted as a place underground with a fiery furnace, I'm led to believe scientists would have seen signs of his existence and residence (Hell) having the available scientific tools for such discoveries.

Many believers of faith subscribe to the worldview that Hell is a terrible place that God cast Satan into and can provide scriptural references to make their case. It is important that we examine how the images and belief of Hell came about. I like to view Hell from a different perspective than the images of a place underground with fire and brimstone in a continuous blaze of punishment for living a sinful life on Earth.

It is true that the Bible does describe Hell as a place that is very hot and where the punished are sent after they die to join Satan for how they lived their life on Earth. Such references in the Bible can be found in Matthew 13:50 were Jesus described the punishment as an unbearable furnace that is full of "wailing and gnashing of teeth." It is important to remember that Jesus spoke in parables, and through examination of all the parables that are recorded in the Gospel books of the Bible, you will notice that each one is symbolic in meaning, filled with hidden messages and not to be taken literally. This parable is no different!

No one can say that a physical place called Hell exists, as I, and many other people who have lost loved ones, have not received a warning to avoid coming where they are if they are in Hell, nor an invitation to come where they are if they are in Heaven. The Bible describes that there is a gulf between the living and the dead (St. Luke 16:26), and it is recommended that we speak that which we do know and testify what our eyes have seen (St. John 3:11). So in reality, no one really knows!

We simply don't know what really happens beyond our fleshly body, but we all have felt unbearable pain, hardships, sickness, worry and death. These and so many other negative circumstances are experiences that we do know and what I like to consider our own personal Hell on Earth. The conditions we experience on Earth can definitely feel like the unpleasant discomfort of Hell, as described by the Bible. These conditions can be seen as a representation of the intense heat from the fire and brimstone, in which some believe that their troubles will never end as a symbolism of "burning forever." Jesus' parable in Matthew 13:50 is not a literal Hell but rather a condition or state of mind during life's toughest moments.

And shall cast them into the furnace of fire: there shall be wailing and gnashing of teeth.

The wailing and gnashing of teeth is symbolic of someone grinding their teeth or the shrilling high-pitched sound of someone using their fingernails to scratch a chalkboard. These sounds are very unpleasant and bothersome to most and illustrate how challenging life can be in comparison to Hell. However, the feeling is a spiritual one that manifests itself in a natural way and not a physical place that we have to die to go to or experience.

When I was miserable, lost and confused during periods of my life, I was in Hell! Life was so dark that I was breathing but far from living. Since Hell is associated with the dead, I knew I was there based on my lifeless state of mind. I had no hope, no direction and ultimately no life. These experiences enlightened me to understand that I don't have to die to experience Hell.

I am not 100% certain that Hell is not a place that sinners go to in the afterlife, and neither is anyone else that is living. As people of faith, we are instructed to believe in the Bible, as it is inspired by God (2 Timothy 3:16). However, it is important that we read the Bible with wisdom and discernment to understand the context the prophets wrote from. As mentioned before, all the books or parables are not to be taken literally, and many are symbolic in meaning.

Overall, Hell is a condition that one does not have to die to experience. The condition is a loss of hope people who have committed or contemplated suicide have experienced. The good news is that the condition does not have to last forever if we choose to see life from an optimistic point of view. The Bible confirms this in Psalms 30:5, which reads, "Weeping may endure for a night, but joy cometh in the morning." When I was at my lowest point in life, I was so glad when my morning came. If you are experiencing a challenging time or situation, refuse to give in and believe your joyful morning is on the way!

THE DEVIL MADE ME DO IT!

We all have heard or maybe even we ourselves have used the catchy phrase, "The Devil made me do it!" Some may see this phrase as an excuse for one's own personal bad judgment, and I will agree that the Devil (negative force) had something to do with it, but I refuse to believe that he made us do it because God gave us the power of choice.

The Devil does not come out of the ground to persuade people to do bad things or cause havoc as some would like to think. Just like God is a spirit and works through human beings while they are living, so does the Devil. We don't have to die to see him in action and can notice his existence in us or in other people's actions and behaviors. Once we recognize the actions and behaviors of the Ruler of Darkness, we then master strategies to avoid Hell and experience the total bliss of Heaven on Earth. It all begins and ends with our state of mind and the desire to choose good and live

(Deuteronomy 30:19). We may not have the power to control the Devil in others, but we do have the power to control the Ruler of Darkness in us.

CHAPTER 4

COPING WITH DEATH

With the death of people close at heart, it can seem nearly impossible to believe in a "Heaven on Earth" concept. Nine months after I decided to move to NY in 1999, I experienced the most horrific tragedy of my life when three members in my family were killed instantly in a car crash. This was no ordinary car crash, and these were no ordinary people. The accident took the life of my mother, my oldest sister and her husband, who was more like a big brother. They were all ordained ministers of our church organization and lost their life in the most unordinary fashion doing a good deed for others as they so often did throughout their lifetimes.

On Christmas day, December 25, 1999, I had just proposed to my present wife at her parents' house which was the day before the accident. Now, living in New York and becoming more acclimated to my new city environment, that Christmas was one of the happiest days of my life. After all the pain and hardship from my first marriage, I was feeling blessed to have found someone that I believed shared my dreams and aspirations to build a future together.

In the company of her family, I waited for the right moment. I asked for everyone's attention and stared her in the face, at the same time, holding out an impressive engagement ring that I had sold my car to buy. I popped the question, "Will you marry me?" Her face lite up and her first response was, "Let me see the size of the ring," then laughed and happily said "Yes!" I was feeling on top of the world, having a second chance at love, and that night the family celebrated the joyous occasion.

The following day, my wife and I gathered at her parents' home after Sunday service like we traditionally did on Sundays. Shortly after our visit, I received a phone call from my brother-in-law at our Brooklyn home with strict, somber instructions. I'll never forget the tone of his voice when the phone was handed to me, and he sternly instructed me to call home. I asked him why, but he wouldn't say and repeated, "Call home!"

We left Manhattan to return to our home in Brooklyn, and I wondered what possibly could be so important that I had to phone home and why my brother-in-law couldn't tell me. I was optimistic that it couldn't be that bad and shocked when I learned the reality of what happened. As I walked in the door, my brother-in-law looked at me with an extremely sad face but spoke no words. I then left their first-floor apartment to go to our home on the second floor to call home. I picked up the phone to speak to my other siblings back home about what possibly could be wrong and received news that forever changed my life.

They told me that I would need to come home immediately as my mother, oldest sister and brother-in-law were all killed in a car accident. I thought it was a joke or at least a dream, but the punch line never came, nor was I sleeping to awaken myself from a dream that couldn't possibly be real. I asked my siblings, "What happened?" and was told a story that would supersede any fiction book.

It was the day after Christmas, Sunday, December 26th, 1999. My mother lived with my sister and brother-in-law in Belleville,

Michigan, and they traveled many places together. Belleville is a country town about 40 miles outside the Detroit city limits, with a number of dirt roads. My oldest sister was always creating special gift items for the church members and gave them out to many in the congregation. After service, they volunteered to take a member home that lived nearby on a dirt road. Their van arrived at her home, pulled in the driveway and dropped her off and watched as she disappeared through her front door.

My brother-in-law (Kenneth) was driving and backed up to the edge of the driveway. Out of nowhere, Kenneth heard a car speeding down the dirt road and stopped the van. While still in the driveway, the speeding car lost control due to the condition of the bumpy road, which forced him to veer off into a fairly deep ditch. Unimaginably, the car went into the ditch and then went airborne as though a rocket shot out of a canon. The speed at which he was traveling after exiting the other side of the ditch forced the car in the air, which landed directly on top of the van my family was driving. They never entered the street, and the force from the impact of the car killed them instantly.

When I returned home, you can imagine the pain, grief and bewilderment that the family was experiencing. After flying back home, I met with two of my brothers, who took me to the spot where it all happened. It just didn't seem real, and at any moment I was hoping to awaken out of my bad dream but never did.

SOMETHING ABOUT 30 YEARS OLD
Since I was 17 years old, I always felt that the age of 30 was going to be a life changing age for me. I was happy to turn 18 and 21, but those monumental years of my life didn't appeal to me as much as the age of 30 and at the time; I didn't understand why. As the family prepared for a three-casket funeral, we had to make a decision about what day the funeral would be. It was the end of 1999, and we didn't want to go into the New Year and have the funerals

after the holiday, so we settled for December 30. As this was the only date that was convenient for all, we moved forward with the planning. At first thought, the planned date for the funeral didn't dawn on me. As I thought about the date a few hours later, I realized that the funeral would be on my 30th birthday. I then realized that the prophecy that I had been shown about my life changing at the age of 30 had come true.

December 30, 1999, was not only the day of the funeral but also the day of my 30th birthday. Sitting in the front pew staring at three caskets on my birthday is forever engrained in my mind. It was the worst birthday I have ever experienced, and that day really was the day that changed my life forever. The spirit of God revealed to me early in life that my 30th birthday would be something monumental, but I had no idea that I would lose so much and feel so much pain on my so-called special day.

LOSING MY BROTHER, MY FRIEND:

While I was near completion of this book, I had to go back and include another unfortunate loss to our family that happened just a few weeks back. My dear brother and good friend died of cancer not long after his diagnosis at only 48 years old. This was a traumatic blow against my heavenly experience on Earth, as my brother and I had a great relationship. We trusted each other, and he always wanted to see me succeed.

Growing up, he was my protector and teacher. He was one who lived more of a so-called "street" lifestyle, yet he shared all his mistakes with me so that I would not follow down the same wrong path. I was nowhere near an angel, but I was known as the church son while Jesse was the one who liked to take more risks in life and built quite a reputation for being very tough. As the youngest of nine siblings, I had to learn to fight; however, my brother's reputation made it possible so that I didn't have to fight at all. Those who knew that Jesse was my brother steered clear of any conflict with me because our dad taught us to stand up for one another, and he did just that and more for my sister and me, all being close in age.

As it has been less than a month since his death, I'm still recovering from the loss but have some comfort knowing that he and I had a great relationship that superseded our blood-line relationship. I was fortunate to have a brother and a friend all in one. At present, I feel a piece of me is missing from his loss, yet the tears I cry are not from guilt or a need to have said or done something to or for him while he was alive.

The tears I cry are strictly out of a place of missing a loved one as opposed to some negative feeling based on what I could have or should have done differently. Just as I internalized my father, mother, oldest sister and brother-in-law to feel their presence, in time I will heal from my loss and give Jesse a home in me, as spirits never die. I will find a way to manage his passing because I still believe the Creator's will is that we live and prosper despite my own personal experiences.

THE CREATOR'S WILL IS THAT WE LIVE AND PROSPER

Despite my own misfortune on the passing of my kinfolk and loved ones, God's will is that we live and prosper. As an ordained minister, I have not only attended many funerals, but have also administered my share of eulogies for the bereaved families. This is the time to mourn the loss and provide strength and encouragement to the family. From my own personal experience with death at such an extreme level, some are surprised at my ability to do other people's funerals, while others think that my expertise qualifies me as the best person for the job.

Jesus' ascension from the dead by the Father further illustrates God's master plan to live. This miracle is one of the pillars of Christianity and further confirmation that God is in the business of life not death. Romans 8:1 reads:

> *But if the Spirit of him that raised up Jesus from the dead dwell in you, he that raised up Christ from the dead shall also quicken your mortal bodies by his Spirit that dwelleth in you.*

According to this scripture, Jesus rise from the dead through the power of the Creator is proof that He is the author of life; otherwise there would be no need for Jesus to be raised from the dead. Furthermore, the passage provides insight that the spirit that raised Jesus from the dead is the same spirit that helps us to prevent death (quicken your mortal bodies). Pay special attention to the end of the verse, as it tells us where God's spirit dwells, which is in us.

Despite the numbers of people who die every day, death was not in the plan of God at the beginning. If we can master God's spirit in our mortal bodies through kingdom living and repentance, similar to his son Jesus, then we have the ability to execute His master plan in our lives on Earth. God is about life, and according to 2 Peter 3: 9, he has no desire that we should perish but live led by repenting and a pure heart.

> *The Lord is not slack concerning his promise, as some men count slackness; but is longsuffering to us-ward, not willing that any should perish, but that all should come to repentance.*

So why does God get the blame when the above reference and so many other scripture passages clearly illustrate God's will is that we live and not die?

WHY DOES GOD GET THE BLAME?
No one can say exactly why a baby dies or why some unfortunate accident may happen, such as what happened to my family that ends in tragedy. While these unfortunate circumstances cannot always be explained as to how or why, it still doesn't mean that God

did it. Many of the things that happen to people in today's world come from a result of our and other people's poor choices.

As we were given dominion over the Earth, our job was to properly care for and live according to God's plan to enjoy His creation. Some of our circumstances are the results that really have nothing to do with us but rather are based on the actions of others centuries or decades before our existence.

Pollution, global warming, parent's sickness passed on to children and many other tragic incidents are all examples of poor choices or lack of knowledge that affect us all. It is important to remember that God set everything in motion at the beginning and many things happen as a result of our negligence as a society. Yet somehow, God gets the blame because we fail to properly exercise our God-given authority on Earth.

The theological belief that when someone dies "God took them" is a belief that I always found disagreeable to what I have learned about the Creator. First and foremost, He is the Creator of Life, so how did He become associated with death, when death was not in the plan for mankind at the beginning?

There are numerous scripture references that expose the true character of God, which is Life. After receiving the gift of life, we were granted authority over the Earth and the power of choice. Deuteronomy 30:19:

> *I call heaven and earth to record this day against you, that I have set before you life and death, blessing and cursing: therefore choose life that both thou and thy seed may live:*

Another reference can be found in Ezekiel 18:31-32 which states,

> *Cast away from you all your transgressions, whereby ye have transgressed; and make you a new heart and a new spirit: for why will ye die, O house of Israel?*

For I have no pleasure in the death of him that dieth, saith the Lord GOD: wherefore turn yourselves, and live ye.

From the above passage and many others, it is clear that God's will is not death but life. If death was not in the plan at the beginning, I have to believe that it is not God who does the killing! From this revelation, we must now ask ourselves, "If not God, then who is in charge of the death department?"

If God is not in charge of this department and represents life, then it would be safe to assume that it would be the opposite of God, known as the Ruler of Darkness or Satan/Devil, as explained in St. John 10:10 -

The thief cometh not, but for to steal, and to kill, and to destroy: I am come that they might have life, and that they might have it more abundantly.

Based on the above passages, I'm amazed how we credit God for when people die as though we are doing Him a favor. This type of theology does not align with God's character as referenced in the Holy Bible. In fact, St. John 3:16 explains how He created His Son and put Him on a special task. This special task was about life, and according to the scripture, the ultimate goal was not just life, but everlasting life.

For God so loved the world that he gave his only begotten Son, that whosoever believeth in him should not perish, but have everlasting life.

If the Father was all about life and He sent his son, Jesus Christ, as an example of life, let's examine what Jesus Himself said about life in St. John 5:24:

Verily, verily, I say unto you, He that heareth my word, and believeth on him that sent me, hath everlasting life, and shall not come into condemnation; but is passed from death unto life.

If we continue to look in the same book of St. John, when Jesus was speaking to the Jewish leaders of his time, you will notice another reference by Jesus, which clearly shows that Jesus was about life and not death. St. John 8:51:

Verily, verily, I say unto you, If a man keep my saying, he shall never see death.

If these references are true, then we should no longer blame God for what He didn't do. It is not God's will that we should die or be unhappy, and He is not the reason for our afflictions, hardships or even death. Often, our circumstances are the results of our choices, and this truth can be found in Romans 8:23.

For the wages of sin is death, but the gift of God is eternal life in Christ Jesus our Lord.

We don't invite death, as death will take care of its own. It you don't believe that's true, then stop eating and drinking water, as death will naturally happen. It's in our human nature to live, and we discover this life-sustaining power in the face of some unimaginable situations and circumstances. No one in their right mind really wants to die, as that would be too easy. From a common-sense perspective and for those of you who know about uninvited house guests like roaches, you will notice how fast they move to hide when you turn on the light. This is simply because even the cockroach wants to live and not die. So why are we so quick to accept death having more intelligence than a cockroach?

I've heard a number of preachers who preach about the glory of dying and going to Heaven, but when they themselves get sick, why are they so quick to call a doctor or seek medical treatment? Truth is, they don't want to die. It's not a fight to die; the only fight we should fight is to live. According to St. Matthew 12:27, Jesus reminds us that God is a god of the living not the dead and we should no longer accept that it's God's will that we die, especially if you believe He sent His son to show us how to obtain everlasting life.

WHAT HAPPENS WHEN WE DIE

Should we fail to reach the goal from a fleshly perspective, it's important to know what happens to our spirit if it doesn't go up to the place known as Heaven in the sky. Ecclesiastes 12:7 explains that the fleshly part returns to Earth while the spirit returns to God.

Then shall the dust return to the earth as it was: and the spirit shall return unto God who gave it

The next question we need to ask is, "Where is God?" As previously referenced, St. Luke 17:21 clearly conveys that the kingdom of God is within you, and I Corinthians 3:16 explains that the temple of God is our bodies. The flesh may perish, but the spirit lives on in living bodies (Heaven in you). The spiritual attributes of those who transitioned from their earthly temple does not end with the loss of the physical house. Their characteristics will continue to be a representation of that person and will often come to memory to those who see or feel a similar spiritual vibration from individuals who are still living or even within oneself. A person who is loving, kind, generous or exhibits other fruits of the spirit (Gal. 5:22-23) only loses the shell should they die and not their spiritual attributes or characteristics. This concept may be hard for some to grasp if looking from a natural rather than a spiritual perspective.

The attributes and characteristics of a person are not limited to any one individual and will continue to be displayed in other living bodies on the Earth. How many times have you run into someone that reminded you of someone else based on their mannerisms, speech or behaviors? Many will agree that the similarities of characteristics from someone that passed can be highly visible in others who are still living. That's because we are spirit beings housed in an outer shell and will continue to exist. As spirit-beings, should we lose the natural house, I believe that it's impossible to recognize loved ones in the flesh, as the flesh returns to the dust of the Earth. However, from a spiritual level, when I see someone who does similar acts or displays similar behaviors of someone who passed, I understand that the person who lost the outer shell is still alive. I just don't have the physical pleasure to enjoy them as I once did, but I still very much feel their continual presence.

WHAT HAPPENS TO OUR LOVED ONES WHEN THEY DIE?
Another widely misinterpreted scripture that I often hear others repeat can be found in 2 Corinthians 5:8, when the author Paul writes:

> *We are confident, yes, well pleased rather to be absent from the body and to be present with the Lord.*

My first question to anyone who mentions this quote is, "Why do we have to die to be present with the Lord? Why can't we be present with Him while we are alive in these bodies, as we are spiritual beings housed in natural bodies or 'tents,' as Paul described them?"

I Peter 2:24 explains the type of death we should seek to obtain while we are alive, and this type of death does not refer to a physical death but rather from sin.

> *He himself bore our sins in his body on the tree, that we might die to sin and live to righteousness. By his wounds you have been healed.*

This makes sense because if we die from sin and live for righteousness, we should have no fear of death, for the wages of sin is death, but the gift of God is eternal life (Romans 6:23). Once we embody the spirit of Christ, we live for righteousness to glorify God in our earthly bodies, and the old things or old ways pass away to welcome a new life (2 Corinthians 5:17).

Many interpret 2 Corinthians 5:8 as though it's an honor to be absent from the body (die) believing that they will be with the Lord. If you read the chapter beginning at the 1st verse of 2 Corinthians 5, you will notice that Paul was not glorifying death as some would like to think. In actuality, Paul was conveying the message that should you lose your earthly body, God has ordained another house, not made by man's hands, and eternal in Heaven (2 Corinthians 5:1).

The "building from God" that the writer speaks of does not support the claim that we will be in God's presence should we die. The alternative way to see this passage is that should we lose our body, we take on a different body, meaning spiritual characteristics of passed loved ones will continue to live on in our bodies or other people's physical bodies. This meaning is much different than a disembodied spirit that lives on after death in the atmosphere, as some would like to think.

Since God is a spirit and He made us in His image and likeness, then it's safe to assume they we too are spirit beings, housed in a body of flesh. Having the experience of losing three people at one time is extremely painful. I still have times when I miss my loved ones physical presence 18 years later. Although painful, the ability to continue to move forward with life without being bitter happened when I embraced the philosophy that they will always live in me. My mentor and spiritual father, Bishop Allen Cox, taught me something that helped me to release the pain from the physical loss of my loved ones by a parable he shared for me to best comprehend the reality of losing a loved one.

When my family was killed, I was numb for months thereafter and didn't know what to believe about God, life or death. In his infinite wisdom, Bishop Cox explained a perspective that has stayed with me and comforted my soul to live again up to this very day. He started with a statement and said, "Imagine if you had a really good friend and one day a fire consumed his home and he had no place to stay." He then asked the question, "As a really good friend, will you let them stay with you?"

When I realized that God is a spirit and we too are spiritual beings, then the parable made a lasting impact on the level of loneliness and sadness I experience from their physical loss. Allowing their spirit to live in me, I realize that in actuality, they still live. They live on whenever I stand for strong causes to fight injustice for others as they so often did. They live when I selflessly help people and share a kind word with anyone in need, and in so many other characteristics that represent who they were. I now understand that they now operate in my life not from the physical plane but from the angelic plane.

ANGELIC POWER

I believe in angels. The Bible describes angels as spiritual beings created by God for special tasks from both the heavenly and natural plane. The word "angel" is derived from the Greek word *aggelos*, which means "messenger." Although the Bible does not share the historical beginnings of angels, it is my belief that they were in attendance with God during creation. According to the story of creation, man was the last thing God created, and in Genesis 1:27, you will notice that God used some help when he said, "Let us make man." It is my belief that the co-creators with God were spirits from the angelic plane.

There are a number of references in the Bible that speaks about the angels, and although the Bible speaks about a "host of angels," very few of them are mentioned by name such as Gabriel and Michael. You will find names of other angels in other historical books like the Apocryphal Book of Tobit, which mentions the angel Raphael, and the archangel Uriel in the Book of Enoch. What I find most intriguing is that even Satan himself was an angel of God before his dissension from the heavenly plane.

Before Satan or Lucifer aligned himself on the side of evil, he was one of God's most beautiful and powerful angelic beings. According to Isaiah 14:12-18, Satan was cast out of the heavenly realm and cursed due to his greed, pride and desire to be as powerful as God instead of a servant of God.

The Bible mentions both good and bad angels that still very much exist today. The good angels are there to protect and guide us through life (light) while the negative angels' job is to make life difficult or take life altogether (dark). Additionally, it's important to know that angels don't have natural wings, and the images that have been created of their appearance are simply not true. Despite John's vision in Revelations 4:8, which mentions angels having six wings, keep in mind that most parts of this book is a book of symbolism with hidden meaning.

If an angel is a spirit, I question the need for wings, not having a permanent physical body, although they are able to take on human form for various causes. I also question that if they did have wings, why would it take six wings for them to fly when a 747 airplane only has two wings? If you read Zechariah 2:3-4, you will notice how the passage speaks of angels in human form that first spoke with the prophet Zechariah and then went out to meet another angel. Notice how the fourth verse instructs the angel to run, not fly, which provides insight for us to understand the reality of angels.

And, behold, the angel that talked with me went forth, and another
angel went out to meet him,
And said unto him, Run

These are thoughts to ponder so that we do not buy into or promote fiction, but rather use our intelligent mind to understand the angelic plane. As angels are spiritual beings and made for our protection and guidance, they operate as God, through bodies. Everything we need or want doesn't just fall out the sky in our laps. Even if you were in need of money and found it on the ground, God didn't drop it out the sky. The money was there because somebody dropped it. In the New Testament, Paul understood how God manifests himself in bodies when he appealed to the people of Rome in Romans 12:1 which reads:

> *I beseech you therefore, brethren, by the mercies of God, that ye present your bodies a living sacrifice, holy, acceptable unto God, which is your reasonable service.*

The angel's assistance in life helps make it possible to live the best quality of life to represent the Creator in the best light possible, as we were created for His glory (Isaiah 43:7). God is a God of the living and desires to use living people so that He may be glorified through our communication and behaviors.

HOST OF ANGELS

> *Suddenly a great company of the heavenly host appeared with the angel, praising God and saying (St. Luke 2:13).*

Just as the Bible mentions a host of angels, we too should build and identify a host of Angels. After losing three family members at one time, I received a revelation from God nearly a year after their death. As I was mentally and spiritually recovering from the loss, I heard a word from Heaven (in me), which spoke to me as though it was a physical human being standing nearby. I was in so much pain, but the voice penetrated my battered spirit and told me that my family would always be with me, except they would be with me on the angelic plane. I then began to wonder how they would be with me and how would I know if they are there or not.

That's when I once again heard a voice from Heaven (in me), and the spirit of God revealed how the loss of the physical is not the end of the individual. The voice reminded me that they are in Heaven, which is in you (St. Luke 17:21), so how can they leave or forsake you? I sat there amazed at what I had just heard. Once I accepted the revelation, my life began to look much brighter than it had in a long time.

The pain that I had felt from losing our family leaders so tragically began to ease almost instantly. I then realized that I am not alone and have a team (host) willing to come to my rescue whenever there is a need. I like to visualize my host as the Verizon wireless commercial which promotes a whole network of people following the subscriber's every move to ensure the best quality phone service is maintained. I have a host of angels at my disposal.

Angels can be used for many things, such as direction, healing and protection; however their main purpose is to serve and make life manageable for the living. This point is made very clear according to Hebrew 1:14:

> *Are they not all ministering spirits sent out to serve for the sake of those who are to inherit salvation?*

This passage further illustrates God's purpose for humankind to live joyously and prosperously on Earth. Knowing that life can be a challenge, He sent help to make the goal of Heaven on Earth a possibility. If you notice, the angel's job aligns with God's master plan, which is to make life a heavenly experience for the living and add to our daily salvation or quality of life.

MY HOST OF ANGELS OR NETWORK

My father, mother, oldest sister, brother-in-law and brother were all instrumental figures that contributed to my growth in life but are no longer physically alive. As previously stated, my father passed when I was 14, I lost the other three leaders of the family at one time nearly 18 years ago, and most recently, I lost my brother and friend, Jesse. Despite the loss, I remain optimistic and I chose to use my circumstances as a motivator instead of circumstances which hinder or block my forward progress.

I accepted the reality that my deceased loved ones are no longer physically here and see them as my own personal angels. This angelic benefit is available to all of us, and if you can tap into a higher level of our heavenly mind, you too will see that you have personal angels waiting to serve and protect you. The physical presence of our loved ones is comforting because we can see them with our physical eyes to know that they are there. Once you fully elevate your mind to the heavenly plane, you will feel the vibration of your personal angels in your spirit and discover that they can do so much more for you now than when they were alive. As they are spirit beings not confined to a physical body, they are at our service 24/7 and don't require the sleep or rest that is required in the physical plane. I can call my angels any day or time and feel their vibration in my spirit and I use each one of them for certain things.

MY ANGEL JAMES

My father was one of the strongest men I knew! As a child, I saw him display some incredible acts of strength that made me see my dad as a superhero. I will never forget how he would impress us (the children) around the 4th of July when he would take some firecrackers and light them while in his hand but never release them. They would go off in his hand and he would stand there like nothing ever happened. One day my brothers and I thought that we could do what Dad did and hold a lit firecracker in our hand. The results were very different, as the firecrackers exploded and my hand required some serious medical attention.

I share this story to convey the purpose my dad plays in my life despite being physically absent from the body for over 30 years. He is my strength! When I need a surge of energy or am faced with some serious physical challenges that require great strength, I call my dad and feel his vibration in my spirit to prove to me that he is there.

Dad was also very handy and could fix nearly anything. I spent the time to observe and assist him fixing many things around the farm and am glad that I inherited his engineering mind. What was most amazing about Dad was how he handled tasks that challenged him. I would watch him spend hours upon hours trying to figure something out, and when he couldn't, he would take a break and sleep on it overnight. During the night, the understanding of how to fix whatever it was that had stunned him would be revealed. By the time I woke up and walked outside, Dad would have the problem resolved.

Today, I use Dad's spirit to help me fix things. When a challenge arises that I don't quite understand how to fix, I step back and leave it for the morning. Coincidentally, when I awake in the morning, the majority of the time I have the answer or receive the insight on how to fix whatever it was that I was uncertain about. James is still very much alive and active in me!

MY ANGEL RUTHIE

My mother was the most amazing woman, and anyone who knew her personally would definitely agree. She was one of the most genuine and kind person that I have ever met. I'm not saying that because she was my mom, but the proof is in the number of adopted spiritual children she acquired during her lifetime. Despite having 10 children of her own, our friends and members of the church considered her their mom just as much as we did being her maternal children.

As the baby of the family, Mom and I shared a very special connection. I knew that she cared for all my other siblings, but she knew how to make each one of us feel uniquely loved. Her generosity and kindness were unparalleled. You could talk to her about nearly anything because she was a very compassionate person and gave sound advice to those who inquired.

At times, when I feel less than perfect and make mistakes, I call my angel Ruthie for reassurance of love and understanding. I use her spirit to avoid being judgmental of others, as Ruthie accepted everyone for who they were. Because of her nonjudgmental ways, so many people sought her out for advice. When I don't feel like being bothered with people or being kind, I call on the spirit of Ruthie to help me reach or maintain a level of compassion for others. Additionally, she was a giver, and I'm also known as a generous giver and I rejoice when others tell me how much I not only resemble her, but how much I act like her. Ruthie is still very much alive in me.

MY ANGEL CHARLENE

Charlene was my oldest sister and was also known as our second mom. As the oldest, she was responsible for assisting our parents with caring for the other siblings, and we respected her just as much as we respected our parents. Charlene was very strong willed and had the gift of prophecy and discernment. Often Charlene would receive visions from God about others and share what she saw. I found her prophetic accuracy quite amazing, as she was always on point when she foretold things about my life. I have been blessed with the same prophetic gift, and I use Charlene's spirit to become a master in discernment to help myself and others just as she so often did.

Also Charlene was extremely creative! Although she was spiritually in tune, she was naturally creative and knew how to make things that people would use or buy. She could take the simplest of objects or items and make them extravagant. When I lack or need creative inspiration, I can call on the spirit of Charlene to always provide the influence to bring out my artistic abilities.

MY ANGEL KENNETH
My brother-in-law Kenneth was like no other man I have met. He was a big man, around 6'4", and although his look could be very intimidating, he had a very pleasant demeanor almost every time you saw him. Kenneth loved to laugh. He always told jokes and was famous for giving others nicknames. My brother-in-law hated to see others sad and would help nearly anyone who needed his help.

Kenneth had a way of making some of the most undesirable moments manageable. He was extremely optimistic, and he serves as my inspiration to laugh! Although I'm a minister that is spiritually in tune, I love to laugh, crack jokes and see others happy just as Kenneth did. Whenever, I'm feeling sad or depressed, I call the spirit of Kenneth to lighten my heavy spirit. Also, when I experience dark moments in my life, I can reflect on one of his jokes or famous sayings to raise my spirit. Kenneth is still very much alive in me and serves as a pivotal source for my optimism and jolly spirit.

MY ANGEL JESSE
Nearly completed with this book, I experienced another unfortunate loss of not only my brother, but my friend. He was two years older than me and passed relatively quickly after being diagnosed with cancer. His death is a tremendous loss because we were very close, and as a big brother, he protected me from so many things.

Jesse didn't start trouble, but he had no problem taking part in it when invited. He was a fighter and extremely "street savvy" and experimented with many things the streets had to offer. Many of the things he learned in the streets he taught me so that I could avoid some of the mistakes he made. I saw him as one who sacrificed many things in his life so that I could have a better one.

Additionally, Jesse was very athletic yet strong willed. When he made up his mind to do or not do something, it was hard to convince him otherwise. After a phenomenal junior year on the high school football team, he decided he didn't want to play football anymore. The high school coaches and players came to our house begging him to play his senior year. He was so good that even the Big Ten coaches from Michigan and Michigan State came to our house to try to convince him to play for them, but he wouldn't budge. He was a running back, and after his junior year, he made up his mind that he didn't want to constantly get hit and risk having a life-changing injury, so he didn't play. The family thought he was making a big mistake, but no matter how much we tried to convince him to take the opportunity, he wouldn't.

My angel Jesse has just joined my network in his recent passing. As I continue to work through the absence of missing his physical body, I'm beginning the process of internalizing him to feel his vibration, just like I can feel the other angels in my network. For me, Jesse represents toughness and a strong will, which are qualities that I need from time to time to overcome some of life's toughest challenges. Even when he was diagnosed with cancer, he didn't complain, and many didn't know he had it because he didn't look sick.

Jesse is the angel that I will use to fight undesirable things and situations that I find myself in. I can call on the spirit of his toughness and strong will to overcome many things that are yet to come my way. Additionally, I will use my angel Jesse to survive potential dangers in places that pose a threat to my well-being. Drawing from Jesse's street knowledge, I'm confident I will feel his vibration of protection and guidance should I need to know exactly what to say or do.

WHO'S IN YOUR NETWORK?

Now that I have shared insight on the angelic plan and my own personal host or network of angels, it's time for you to begin thinking about your network. Similar to the catchy Verizon slogan "Whose in your network?" you should identify your host of angels. Think about the gifts, characteristics and talents of those you have lost that can be beneficial to your own personal needs. As they are spirit-beings and you are a spirit housed in a physical body, you have the ability to commune with them through vibration at any point or given day.

I have learned that the spiritual connection that I share with my lost loved ones helps to manage the level of pain I feel from the physical loss. Feeling their presence provides a sense of comfort from their absence, and rarely do I feel the need to shed physical tears. I realize they are with me and there to do what angels do best: protect and serve.

CHAPTER 5
KEYS TO THE KINGDOM

W hen Jesus got ready to make a transition from his earthly body to complete his mission on Earth, he gave Peter the keys to the kingdom (St. Matthew 16:19)

And I will give unto thee the keys of the kingdom of heaven: and whatsoever thou shalt bind on earth shall be bound in heaven: and whatsoever thou shalt loose on earth shall be loosed in heaven

The keys that Jesus passed on to Peter were not natural keys but rather spiritual keys that represented keys of wisdom, knowledge and understanding. When used properly, these are the keys which give us direct access to the abundance of peace, joy, prosperity and other attributes from the heavenly plane.

Just as Jesus gave some keys to Peter, I see this book as the opportunity to pass along some valuable keys to make the most of your life on Earth. The life of Jesus illustrates the divine connection with the Creator of Life that is now available to you and me. Now that Jesus has finished His work (I have glorified You on the Earth. I have finished the work which You have given Me to do.

St. John 17:4), it's time for us to begin our work so that we too can magnify the Creator of Life through achieving the highest quality of living on Earth.

When you decide to take charge over your life and no longer assume the victim role, The Creator promised that He wouldn't leave us alone to take on the world by ourselves. Jesus prayed that the Father would send a "Comforter" or "Spirit of truth" to take his place in his physical absence, and this spiritual entity of God is always there to assist us and is in us. St. John 14:16-17:

> *And I will pray the Father, and he shall give you another Comforter, that he may abide with you forever; Even the Spirit of truth; whom the world cannot receive, because it seeth him not, neither knoweth him: but ye know him; for he dwelleth with you, and shall be in you.*

My goal for this book was not only to share my life story to inspire others but also provide some keys to gain and maintain a heavenly mindset. To maximize the life experience, I have learned some practices (keys), worth sharing that helps to keep my mind elevated to experience Heaven right here on Earth.

Key #1: Prayer & Meditation

These days we all can appreciate the convenience and rate of speed that technology provides to get things done. Wonderful inventions such as washing machines, microwaves and airplanes provide tremendous time-saving benefits. However, there are two things that we should never rush through. Those things are prayer and meditation.

Many people of faith believe in God but rarely spend the time to pray and meditate. Praying is never the issue for most, and often we pray in the morning while brushing our teeth, cooking breakfast, showering, driving, etc. This type of praying is what I call, "Praying on the go!" and we all are guilty of doing this at one time or another or maybe all the time for some.

Imagine if you had a relationship with someone who you would call your soul mate but you rarely talked to or had a meaningful, heartfelt conversation with. Prayer is the conversation that we initiate with God, and it is important to see the relationship-building aspect with Him through our prayers. Adding meditation to our prayer provides the practice to make those conversations genuine from spending the time to speak to Him in prayer, and He responds to us through our meditation.

We have been taught to pray since youth, but not much time was spent teaching meditation techniques. As a result, many people are unsure of how to meditate. While there are many ways to practice meditation, here are some tips that I use to get you started on your beginner's journey.

1. Get a clear 8-12 oz. glass with no writing or pictures on it.
2. Fill the glass 2/3 with water.
3. Find a quiet place in or around your home.
4. While sitting or standing with both hands cupped around the side of the glass, stare into the center of the glass filled with water.
5. While staring into the glass, begin to recite the 23 Psalms or the Lord's Prayer.
6. Listen to every word you recite and see the words in your mind while constantly staring in the glass of water.
7. Next is the addition of breathing, which provides the mechanism to totally align oneself with the spirit of God through our breaths (The Breath of Life).
8. While reciting your prayer, staring in the glass, slowly breathe in and out, allow your mind to freely experience the moment of things that come. Feel His presence, listen to His voice.

(Example Using the 23rd Psalms}

(While taking in a long, deep breath, say in your mind)
THE LORD IS MY SHEPHERD...
(While exhaling deep and slow, say in your mind) I SHALL
NOT WANT...

(While taking in a long deep breath, say in your mind) HE
MAKETH ME TO LIE DOWN IN GREEN PASTURES...
(While exhaling deep and slow, say in your mind) HE
LEADETH ME BESIDES THE STILL WATERS...

(While taking in a long deep breath, say in your mind) HE
RESTORETH MY SOUL
(While exhaling deep and slow, say in your mind) HE
LEADETH ME IN THE PATH OF RIGHTEOUSNESS

(While taking in a long deep breath, say in your mind) FOR
HIS NAME SAKE
(While exhaling deep and slow, say in your mind) YEA
THOUGH I WALK THROUGH THE VALLEY OF THE
SHADOWS OF DEATH

(While taking in a long deep breath, say in your mind) I
WILL FEAR NO EVIL
(While exhaling deep and slow, say in your mind) FOR
THOU ART WITH ME

(While taking in a long deep breath, say in your mind) THY
ROD AND THY STAFF THEY COMFORT ME
(While exhaling deep and slow, say in your mind) THOU
PREPAREST A TABLE BEFORE ME IN THE PRESENCE
OF MINE ENEMIES

(While taking in a long deep breath, say in your mind) THOU ANOINTEST MY HEAD WITH OIL
(While exhaling deep and slow, say in your mind) MY CUP RUNNETH OVER

(While taking in a long deep breath, say in your mind) SURELY GOODNESS AND MERCY
(While exhaling deep and slow, say in your mind) SHALL FOLLOW ME ALL THE DAYS OF MY LIFE

(While taking in a long deep breath, say in your mind) AND I WILL DWELL IN THE HOUSE OF THE LORD
(While exhaling deep and slow, say in your mind) FOREVER...

Mastering this technique takes practice, so don't be alarmed if you have trouble performing all four things effectively at the beginning. Doing four things simultaneously with precision is a small representation of the mind of God who can do all things, at all times, at the same time.

As you meditate, allow the thoughts to come. It is not uncommon that your thoughts may drift, and during these contemplative moments we commune with a Higher Power through our spirits. Once you have consciously examined the incoming message, return to the prayer and pick up the prayer where you left off and listen for the next message. The more you practice, the easier it gets and the more you will make your prayer and meditation an exhilarating experience.

Prayer & Meditation Continued – The 4-7-8:
One other meditation practice that I use regularly is called the 4-7-8, created by Dr. Andrew Weil. The method is described as a "natural tranquilizer for the nervous system," helping to quickly

reduce tension and allow the body to relax. This exercise is simple, takes almost no time, requires no equipment and can be done anywhere. Although you can do the exercise in any position, it's best to start with the sitting position with your back straight while learning the exercise.

1. While sitting with your back straight, close your eyes and empty all the air from your lungs by exhaling through your mouth/lips in whistle position.
2. Close your mouth and inhale quietly through your nose to a mental count of four.
3. Hold your breath for a mental count of seven.
4. In one breath, exhale completely through your mouth/lips in a whistle position for a mental count of eight seconds.
5. Now inhale again and repeat the cycle three more times for a total of four breaths cycles. If you have trouble holding your breath, speed the exercise up, but keep to the ratio of 4:7:8 throughout the phases. With practice, you can slow it all down and get used to inhaling and exhaling more and more deeply.

This exercise sounds simple, yet it is very powerful. By breathing out chunks of CO_2, the body releases acid, which helps purify the body. According to Dr. Weil, the released acid de-acidifies the body; otherwise the organism has to make "debts" on the body by taking alkaline minerals like potassium, calcium and magnesium out of the bones and muscles to stabilize the pH-value of the blood.

The lack of alkaline minerals in our bodies leads to depression, loss of energy, nervousness and a host of other life-depleting issues. This exercise is good for insomnia, managing stress or anger, and overcoming cravings and addictions. I have personally found great benefits in this exercise to help manage pain.

Key #2: High Energy Vibration

The second key I will share is high-energy vibration. I have learned that, as spirit beings, we operate through vibration and divine energy. According to Eideson (2010), "Everything physically manifested vibrates within certain ranges of frequency in order for human senses to perceive it."

Understanding this key concept provides the consciousness to maintain a positive outlook, knowing that when we vibrate at higher levels, we experience the most joy and peace. When our vibration is low, we experience sorrow and sadness. Generally we allow life circumstances to determine our vibration frequency, but imagine if you found a way to vibrate high despite the things you see, hear or experience. This does not mean that you are heartless or emotionless at the misfortune of self or others, but it means that you have made a conscious decision to remain optimistic and hopeful.

When we enter into a state of fear, worry or anger, we have entered in a low frequency level of vibration or state of darkness. Just as night cannot remain through the rising of the morning sun, we too have the capability to dissipate the dark moments in our lives through the vibration of light we allow to enter into our spiritual and physical bodies.

Living in high-vibration mode also gives one the ability to attract things that vibrate high or have high frequency. Things known as "The Fruits of the Spirit" are attributes that come to those in high vibration mode and include love, joy, peace, patience, kindness, goodness, faithfulness, gentleness and self-control (Galatians 5:22-23). These attributes represent light, and those who consciously fight to maintain these attributes vibrate at a higher level and are not affected by surrounding circumstances or challenges that come.

Those who live in low-vibration mode experience the other side of light, which is darkness or "Works of the Flesh" (Galatians 5:19). These attributes of darkness found in Galatians 5:19-21 include sexual immorality, impurity, idolatry, sorcery, enmity, strife, jealousy, fits of anger, rivalries, dissensions, divisions, envy and drunkenness. Like the Fruits of the Spirit, these attributes attract what they are, except the lower vibration frequency attracts lower vibration attributes. Unlike the law of polarity, in which opposite polar forces attract and similar forces repel, this spiritual law operates from the law of attraction.

Additionally, high vibration provides the emphasis for spiritual discernment and enlightenment from the Creator of Life. How many times have you had a feeling or heard an internal voice that either forewarned you to avoid a certain situation or promoted you to take a certain action? As spirit beings, we all experience these moments, and some experience them more than others because they choose to vibrate at a higher level. We associate terms such as energetic, vibrant, magnetic or prophetic and other terms that represent light with those who choose to vibrate at high levels.

Every day when I wake up, I'm conscious of the level of vibration I choose to operate in. I'm aware that things happen no matter what vibration I may operate in, but I still have the choice to shine my light in dark places. I believe that if I keep my head up despite my situation, I have an opportunity to regain or maintain my heavenly disposition. To do so, one's vibration will need to be connected to a Higher Power, which operates as the generator to our spiritual life source. When I keep my head up, I see what's coming ahead and can take full advantage of things to come. When I walk with my head down, often opportunities are missed because I fail to see further than my situation, and things have a way of passing me by. Until you decide to lift your head up to see what's coming, you will continue to miss your moments to rise above.

Key #3: Planting Good Seeds/Karma
The third key I have learned and will share is the concept of reaping and sowing. Reaping and sowing is one of the oldest, most

well-known sayings in the Bible that many have heard, "for whatsoever a man soweth, that shall he also reap" (Galatians 6:7). This is a key concept for managing things that come your way, so planting good seeds is recommended to reap a good harvest. Some like to see it as Karma, and I believe that although you cannot predict what's to come, you can maximize what's to come by what you plant or put out.

Life can be simple and starts by living by the code of "doing unto others as you would have them do unto you." Jesus referred to this code as "The Golden Rule" (St. Matthew 7:12) and it is one of the master keys that one should adhere to maximize life opportunities.

I make it a daily goal to put out positive, high energy so that I can receive it in return. While this exchange may happen in the spirit world, a simple natural example to help us comprehend this spiritual law is when you say "hello" to someone you encounter. Most people you say "hi or "hello" to will return with a similar response, even if they don't know you, simply because you said it first. Yes, you will get some who may not say "hi" in return, but the majority of people you say "hi" to will acknowledge your greeting and return one to you.

You can agree that someone who exhibits a high degree of love has a higher probability of love being returned because of the spiritual attraction of love. Love recognizes love and peace recognizes peace! This works the same for distributing kind acts, good deeds or positive words. The more you put out, the more you open the doors for their return. The truth remains the same when you put out the opposite, so it is extremely important to be conscious of what you put out or what you plant.

It is important that you know that the laws of reaping and sowing on a spiritual level may differ in comparison to a natural scenario of planting and harvesting. Generally, the place a planter plants the seeds is where the growth and harvest will also take place. This is not always so in the spirit laws of reaping and sowing. Sometimes the good deeds we do for others will be returned but not always by the same person the act was done for.

The spiritual realm of reaping and sowing exceeds the natural realm and is not confined to any particular person for a return. The return in the spirit realm is much bigger, and the seeds we plant can and will come from more than where we have planted the seeds. Some people may never have the ability to give or do for you what you can do for them, but by planting the seeds, those things come back to you from different sources or people. With that in mind, never stop doing for others who don't do the same for you because even though they cannot or won't return what you have shared, the law of reaping and sowing is a spiritual law that ensures your good is never lost. Galatians 6:9: "And let us not be weary in well doing: for in due season we shall reap, if we faint not."

Key #4: Push to Become the Best You

The Creator desires that we become the best that we can be, and in doing so, we represent who He is, as we were made in His image and likeness, created with purpose to glorify the Creator. Isaiah 43:7 reads:

> "Even every one that is called by my name: for I have created him for my glory, I have formed him; yea, I have made him."

The fourth valuable key that I will share is having the mindset to be the best you that you can be. Being the best you is the only requirement necessary for us to live our lives to the fullest. We often fail miserably when we try to be someone or something else that we are not.

The goal to executing this key is learning who you are. It may take some time, but you must know who you are along with your strengths and weaknesses. Take special note of the things that come naturally to you, as these are the things known as gifts from God. The Creator created us all uniquely special, and mimicking others outside our own talent pool only creates a lack of confidence and trust in one's ability.

As an educator, I have learned that most people achieve their goals when they first believe that the goal they have set is reachable. Those who lack confidence or feel inferior to their challenge don't succeed because they first can't conceive that the goal can be reached by their own capabilities. No one is good at everything. Accepting this reality, you align yourself with a spiritual force that can help increase your skill level at what you are good at. We all have room for improvement and maximizing gifts that you do well increases your heavenly experience on earth. This is how you gain confidence to do all things through Christ (Philippians 4:13).

It is extremely gratifying to achieve a goal that you knew would be a challenge but you did anyway. You are empowered with confidence, which is necessary component to have a heavenly experience on Earth because you believe not only in yourself but the Creator's ability to use you for great purpose.

Learn your gifts while setting goals that are reachable. Understanding things that you do well can rid yourself of doubt and fear when setting goals. Maximizing our goals and talents is an intricate part of the heavenly Earth experience, and when we fail to push ourselves to be or do better, than we fall short of heaven's glory.

Based off of the revelation of being the best that I can be, I managed to achieve some amazing things in my life. I had to have confidence and faith in the Creator to move from Michigan to New York. This achievement set the tone for the first of many achievements to come. I now realize that I can survive in the big city, and I adjusted to make the most of my move. Additionally, I learned that you become a byproduct of your environment, and the energy and hustle and bustle of New York provided a hustle and bustle mindset that I had to obtain in order to keep up. Seeing so many people homeless and begging for money is a regular everyday occurrence for me, and that reality pushes me to do what I need to do to avoid a similar fate.

Through accepting the reality of the fatal car accident that ended my kinfolk's physical life, I used that unfortunate circumstance to push me to higher heights and deeper depths in life. After getting over feeling sorry for myself and overcoming the "why me" syndrome, I internalized their spirits, and their vibration served as motivation to do great things. I was no longer living for myself. I was and still am living to represent my fallen family members in my body, and this perspective in return gives me purpose to live. I see my set goals as ways to keep my people alive and I draw from their spirits to achieve those goals and become who I am today.

THE PURSUIT OF EDUCATION

For me, achieving the highest level of education in the academic world is part of my heavenly experience. Since the move to New York, despite the death of loved ones close to me, I now hold some pretty high profile roles and positions. I recently completed my PhD to become a Dr., a lifelong professional dream growing up. I discovered early in life that I was good at counseling and thought I was going to be a psychologist. Although I knew that I would be a doctor someday, I didn't know it would be a doctor of philosophy not psychology. The doctorate of philosophy is the highest doctoral degree even before the field of medicine, and I'm pleased I chose this area of expertise.

As a doctor of philosophy, I have more flexibility and can use my educational background to teach in a college, consult companies in the field of organizational leadership, form a business from my field of study and even write books. I think life as a psychologist would be great but believe that type of occupational field would not offer me as much flexibility to live my professional life to the fullest.

I finally found my way back to college during the second year of my stay in New York and completed the associate degree that I started way back in 1988. When I finally returned to the classroom in 2001, I refused to stop pursuing my college education because I knew how hard it was to get back in school. To live life to the fullest, I believe one must have options and having a PhD gives me just that.

As time went on, I finished my bachelor's degree in psychology from Empire State College, then my master's degree in education from Michigan State University and my PhD in organizational leadership from The Chicago School of Professional Psychology in 2015. I have spent the last 14 years of my life in school and working full time, and I managed to maintain my status as a devoted husband and father and the many other roles that I hold. There were many days that I just didn't get much sleep and learned how to operate on four to six hours of sleep to achieve all that I had to do.

Obtaining my PhD was not an easy task, yet I managed to complete it in five years, attending school year around with only semesters and holiday breaks. I really didn't know what I was getting into at the onset of the program, and there were many times I felt extremely overwhelmed. Despite the 3.8 GPA that I maintained throughout the program, midway through the dissertation process, I failed the competency test requirement. I was extremely disappointed when I learned that I had to travel back to Chicago for a one-day trip just to retest so that I could continue my study. The second time taking the test, I passed, and in November of 2015, my chair and dissertation committee declared me a PhD.

Earning a doctorate degree is one of the highest levels of education in the world, and what the title stands for is much more than prestige or notoriety. I'm proud to have joined the small percentage of world-wide PhD's and the ability to endure the demands and rigor of the degree program and finish is what I value most about the experience. Many people have started in a PhD program but failed to finish. You can complete all the necessary course work required in the program, but without passing the competency test and completing a dissertation, your time, efforts and money spent to get to that doctorial status means little.

One of the concepts that I learned in the program that is applicable to any massive project or goal is called "chunking." Chunking is when you take a step-by-step approach as opposed to a holistic approach to meet your goals. It is when you remain completely focused only with the task at hand without trying to resolve the whole thing. From this approach, you will progressively make steady movements toward your goal in an incremental fashion.

Earning a doctorate degree comes with many steps, and if you don't take a "chunking" approach, the workload requirements on the road to completion can be stressful. Throughout the program, my chair had to periodically remind me to not look at everything as a whole, but learn to complete what's in front of you and complete "chunks" of work at one time as opposed to trying to tackle the whole project.

Learning the skill set of chunking has helped me to manage many large tasks in my leadership role. When I encounter tasks that seem challenging or large in size, I begin the process of chunking and complete one step at a time. As with my PhD program of study came to an end, so too will any task that I'm faced with as long as I take it piece by piece and refuse to quit. The same will happen to you if you apply the same concept.

CHALLENGE YOURSELF TO LEARN A NEW SKILL OR HOBBY THAT CHALLENGES YOU

Learning a new hobby or skill that you are passionate about provides a richer feel to your heavenly experience. Another great achievement that happened in the first year after I moved to New

York was when I learned to play the piano. Although I have some knowledge of the piano scale, I play by ear and inherited the role of minister of music at my local church.

When I moved to New York, the church did not have any music for the service. Coming from a church with several sets of musicians, choirs and groups, having no music didn't feel right to me, so I volunteered to learn. I borrowed a keyboard from one of the church members and set on a journey to learn how to play. Being self-taught was a challenge, but I didn't give up and can play most songs that I hear for the first time in the gospel genre. I don't consider myself a classical piano genius, but knowing that I was able to pick up the skill of piano playing provides confidence that I can do anything that I set my mind to.

From this experience, I learned that everyone should explore a hobby that they like and also challenges them. So often we are passionate about something but lack the perseverance or courage to master our passion if met with uncertainty or lack of confidence. Stepping out of your comfort zone is a requirement for growth, and if we take a "chunking" approach and have faith in a Higher Power, we are assured to succeed. When faced with any mountain, if you are willing to raise your white flag in submission to His will and not your situation, you will find great strength to overcome. With God as your partner, it's time to make your plans larger.

MINISTRY

If you discover your life calling, it's much easier to stay focused on your goal when challenges come. A few months after the tragic accident, I was given a chance to be called to the ministry to continue the family legacy of ministry in honor of my fallen family members. I served as a reverend for many years and then was awarded an opportunity to become an assistant co-pastor in 2010. In 2012, my senior pastor decided to retire from her role as pastor, and I was afforded an opportunity to serve as co-pastor of the church in Harlem and recently ordained as an elder in June of 2016.

My role as pastor is further confirmation of why I believe my arrival to New York was predestinated and not by accident. Some question my motivation for being a minister when three of my fallen family members were ministers who died in a car crash. From that perspective, the call of ministry does not sound all that appealing; however my motivation for ministry is based on my life calling in ministry. I knew early in my adolescent years that I would one day be a minister but had no idea it would be in the role of a co-pastor in Harlem, New York.

I learned that it takes a special person to effectively pastor a church, and often your immediate family has to sacrifice just as much, if not more, then the pastor. I always say that preaching behind a pulpit only accounts for 10% of the work that a pastor must do. The majority of the time is spent counseling, visiting the sick and incarcerated, being available at any time of day or night for phone calls, performing weddings and funerals and participating in many charitable events.

I knew early in life that I would be a minister, coming from a family of ministers, and all of the hardships, trials and tribulations that I experienced in my lifetime prepared me to be the best pastor I can be. To make connections with those who come to me for counsel, I always find ways to share pieces of my life when necessary to show that no matter what you have been through; God can use you as an example to help others if you are willing to be used.

One valuable tip that I have learned about ministry is that it is not confined to just reverends or preachers. Ministry is a practice that anyone at any level or social status can do because it's based on the ability and willingness to help those in need. Helping those in need comes in many forms and extends much further beyond a message from the pulpit. In that sense, I was a minister long before I was a church-ordained elder, and this concept applies to all of us.

The last and perhaps the boldest perspective I will share regarding my own personal ministry is taking pride in exercising the ministry that the Creator of Life gave me to fulfill. We all have a ministry, and if you try to judge me by what societal standards define as a ministry, you will find that I don't fit that box, and I take pride in not doing so. I have no problem sharing with others that I'm not your so-called average minister or pastor, and the approach of being able to relate to people's imperfections, on their level, has been my strength in building a meaningful network of like-minded individuals and following.

My prayer for this book is that it will minister to those who are hurting and finding difficulty dealing with so many daily tragedies, not only in the world, but first and foremost in their own personal communities and families. It is my hope and prayer that my perspective or ministry regarding Heaven and Hell on Earth has challenged our traditional world view of Heaven and Hell to see what actions we can take now to enjoy paradise on Earth instead of waiting to die and go to it.

MY PROFESSIONAL LIFE

To experience the fullness of God's Heaven on Earth, I desired to have a life outside of my church life. I personally feel that building our professional life outside our church life is equally important to our heavenly experience on Earth. If you can find the means to encompass both in one and make a comfortable living doing so, then you are really on the right track to the open windows of Heaven.

I have been blessed to work in a collegial academic environment for more than 14 years. Since my move to New York, I have worked at three different colleges and held the role of associate director for more than 10 years. When I first moved to New York, my career started at a temp agency. I got my foot in the door of a college as an office coordinator and was later hired fulltime by the college as a career counselor. After two years in that role, I was offered a chance to fill a newly appointed position as coordinator of online learning. That was the start of not only my online professional career but also the methodology that provided the means for me to manage a work, life and school balance.

Not only was I an online administrator during the past 10 years of my life, I was also an online student and I'm grateful for online education. As an expert in the field, I do realize that taking class online is not for everyone. It requires the ability to be an independent learner with great time management skills, yet it is perfect for the person with a busy or demanding schedule looking for a way to go back or continue their education. Having such positive online experiences, I would rather take a course online any day than sit in a classroom. I encourage any working adult to not be afraid of going back to school. Online education is not only a credible way to learn but also provides the means to continue or complete an educational dream.

I'm proud of the professional roles that I hold and the ability to simultaneously maintain them effectively. I continue to find ways to balance my home, school, church and professional life since my move to NYC, and now I'm starting to reap all the benefits from my hard work. To achieve such balance is no easy task, but if you are willing to put in the work, in time you will see your progress.

NEW BUSINESS OWNER

Being the best me that I can be also includes being a self-proprietor and build my own business instead of working for others to help them build theirs. In my doctorial study, I chose to explore a topic that is relatively new in a traditional organizational leadership PhD program. The topic I studied was workplace spirituality, and my research explored the new emerging management paradigm called workplace chaplaincy. My study required me to travel to Madison, Wisconsin, after connecting with business owners and workplace chaplains in the area to learn how the business concept works in a traditional business environment opposed to a religious organization.

After learning more about workplace chaplaincy, halfway through my doctorate program, I knew that this type of business was ideal for me. As a pastor, I spends so much of my time in service to others, and so this type of business seemed like it was tailored made just for me. I understand that ministry is my calling, but not in the traditional sense of ministry. I'm attracted to this business because it allows me to minister to others beyond the church walls without pushing any religion on anyone, not even my own. To learn more about Workplace Chaplain Services, LLC., please see the appendices section and visit my website http://wpcs.us/.

Another entrepreneur victory happened when my wife and I were approved to open up Mz. Lynn's Day Spa and Salon in Bayside, New York. Owning a spa and salon has been a life-long dream of my wife and after graduating from college with an MBA and then pursing her passion; she attended cosmetology school.

After graduating at the top of her class, she put in the research and the work to open up her own salon less than a year after graduation. Seeing her lifelong dreams becoming reality provides further proof that Heaven is within our reach. In as sense, setting goals is no different than taking a road trip. You decide where you going, look at the map for direction, follow the map, and then drive the distance. Following these steps will help you reach your destination and arrive at the front door of any goal that you are sincerely passionate about.

MY DAUGHTERS

Of all the accomplishments in my life that I am most proud of, the re-establishment and building of relationships with my three daughters rank at the top. The roles and promotions I received may sound impressive to some, but they came with a big price tag. I had to endure being an inactive physical presence in my daughter's life the first few years of my stay in New York. I would write often and try to call as much as possible, but none of that took the place of seeing them grow up on a daily basis.

After my present wife and I got married, I was blessed with the opportunity to have the two youngest girls move with us to New York during their middle school years. I prayed for the opportunity to be a daily part of their life, and although I was extremely excited for the opportunity, it came with much hardship. I quickly learned that raising two young girls in NYC can seem like a parent's worst nightmare if plagued by constant worry and stress. They were raised in a suburban environment with roughly 300-400 children in a school and came to a New York City school with an enrollment of over 4,000 students in one school. The majority of the one million population of public school students ride city buses and trains to get back and forth, and you can imagine the daily pandemonium my wife and I felt every day that they had to go to school. This was an experience that was new for all of us, and I'm so grateful to have made it through those tough times.

After they moved to New York at the ages of nine and eleven, we experienced the parent/step-parent/children challenge and often we didn't see eye to eye. There were many days that I had no solution to some of the problems, and I felt overwhelmed on a number of occasions. The older they got, the more conflicting seeing eye-to-eye became, and New York is not the place to live without everyone being on the same page.

After living in New York for more than five years during their high school years, I decided that it was best that they return to Michigan. In retrospect, I can admit that every family challenge we had as a family was not their fault, and sometimes I made bad decisions or none at all. Despite not knowing what to do at times, I did know that New York is not the place for family units to not be on the same page having so many outside distractions. The forced move caused a lot of dissension between the girls and I because they really liked New York. Nonetheless, I knew in my spirit that the city of New York was not the best place for them to continue their education.

Despite the hurt feelings caused when I decided it was time for them to return back to Michigan, I prayed one day that they would grow to understand why such a hard decision had to be made. They would eventually complete high school and go on to college and now are young ladies in their 20's. They now have the opportunity to make New York their permanent home. We all found a way to move beyond our hurtful past and share a special relationship now that they are young adults. They now value the experience of growing up in New York for most of their school years, and that experience afforded them an opportunity to experience diversity in a city like no other. Now they are trendsetters, adventurous and willing to take risks outside of their own comfort zone. I know New York had a lot to do with who they are today, and I wanted to make sure my children see more than the dirt roads I grew up on in Maybee, Michigan.

Additionally, my oldest daughter and I also repaired our broken relationship after many years of not communicating. Several years ago, we reconnected and that was the first time I met my two beautiful grandchildren. When she decided to get married, she asked if I would do the honor of giving her away. I was humbled, and although I'm not her biological farther, she told me that I was the only father she had ever known and would ask to give her away. The wedding turned out great, and I'm very proud of my new son-in-law. Now she has given birth to my third granddaughter, I'm excited to be a grandfather and a part of their lives. God promised He would put the pieces of my life back together if I made Him my priority. I did and will continue to do just that, and having meaningful relationships with my daughters makes life on Earth fabulous.

PUBLISHED AUTHOR

What are your wildest dreams? I have always had some decent writing skills, but I never imagined that I would become a published author. Despite the challenge of becoming a published author, I never allowed myself to believe that I couldn't if I put my mind to it. The skills I adopted when learning how to play the piano and complete a doctorate program of study are skills that are transferrable to any part of my life for achieving success.

Just like the story of Moses we covered in previous chapters, I was very apprehensive regarding my writing and lacked the confidence to think that I could ever write and publish a book. The PhD program I completed helped me to overcome my fear of writing, and this book is my second published work.

Writing a book can be an overwhelming experience, and attacking such a project without "chunking" only makes the task more challenging. Additionally, writing a book is a step-by-step process in which every book starts with writing one page at a time. You must pick a topic that you are very knowledgeable about, and one that stirs up passion as these requirements will allow you to keep pushing forward to completion. Now as a published author, I'm amazed when I start to write without focusing on the number of pages, how the pages just seem to add up and turn into chapters. One of the joys of writing for me is the opportunity to capture my thoughts on paper and see them take shape and grow, which is an exhilarating heavenly experience.

Being a published author provides the ability to not only share my thoughts with the world but to also have a profession that I can continue long after my retirement years. Also, I see writing as a vehicle for me to brand myself through book signings, workshops, public speaking and hopefully the opportunity to appear on radio/TV. Ultimately, being a published author provides a chance for me to continue my legacy. Should I one day loose this natural house, my recorded words and thoughts will never die, which is one way I believe I will live forever.

Key #5: CHOOSE LIFE AND LIVE

The fifth and final key I will share is to choose life and live! The main objective of this book is to provide not only encouragement but enlightenment that challenges our traditional beliefs and examines our present experience through living in the moment. While the promise of an afterlife in Heaven is very appealing, we must make our earthly experience a heavenly one. Despite our own human incapability to know what lies ahead for us in the spirit world should we lose the earthly shell, the power of choice is the only power that we do have control over. The dominion given to Adam at the beginning of creation was also extended to Moses and the children of Israel. This is the same dominion that is now extended to us today, and we have the authority to choose.

Deuteronomy 30:15-16

> *See, I have set before thee this day life and good, and death and evil;*
> *In that I command thee this day to love the* Lord *thy God, to walk*
> *in his ways, and to keep his commandments and his statutes and*
> *his judgments, that thou mayest live and multiply: and the* Lord
> *thy God shall bless thee in the land whither thou goest to possess it.*

Making decisions and choices is inevitable and something we are required to do so every day of our life. Even if you decided to lie in bed and do nothing, you made a choice. Our choices extend to acts and behaviors that we sometimes unconsciously make without any effort, and we have the choice to decide whether we should smile or frown, laugh or cry, or ultimately do good or evil.

This book is to empower us to lose the expectancy of a mystical magic wand used by the Creator of Life that will cure all of our problems through one simple wave in our direction. This fallacy simply does not exist! It takes work to reach and remain in Heaven. Deuteronomy 30:16 mentions the work it takes to experience Heaven on Earth, and the experience requires actions that complement our power of choice. It starts with acknowledging a power greater than yourself that operates on the spiritual plane to make life a fuller, richer experience. The power transcends our beings and unlocks the hidden treasure of life to experience paradise on Earth if we can see life through a different worldview than what we have heard or been taught.

As previously mentioned, no one knows what happens to us should we lose our physical bodies. However, it is my belief that if there is an afterlife in Heaven, it has to start here on Earth. I'm convinced that if I live a heavenly experience on Earth (positive, charitable, kind, optimistic, etc.), should there be an afterlife Heaven as depicted by so many believers of Heaven, then my probability of reaching Heaven after death greatly increases. You can't live wrong and expect a good end, but if I practice a morally conscious lifestyle and use the keys that I have been given, I increase my chances of experiencing what I call a "double-Heaven" experience from both a natural and spiritual level. Should there be no afterlife Heaven experience, then to experience Heaven on Earth is the ultimate earthly reward. In contrast should there be a spiritual afterlife in Heaven, I believe if I can get it right on Earth, I have no doubt I can get it right in Heaven—especially when you know that Heaven is in you.

SCRIPTURE REFERENCES

GENESIS
1:8
1:20
1:26
1:27
2:22
3:24

EXODUS
4:10
14:13
14: 15-16

DUETERONOMY
10:14
30: 11-14
30:15-16
30:19

ISAIAH
14:12-18
26:3

40: 26

43:7

EZEKIEL

18:31-32

PSALMS

30:5

51:10

ECCLESIATES

12:7

ZECHARIAH

2:3-4

MALACHI

3:10

ST MATTHEW

6:10

7:12

10:7

12:27

13:50

16:19

ST MARK

10:18

ST LUKE

2:13

8:21
16:26
17:21

ST JOHN
1:1
1:14
3:11
3:16
4:24
5:24
7:38
8:51
10:10
14:16-17
17:4

ROMANS
6:23
8:11
8:23
12:1
14:17- 18

1 CORINTHIANS
3:16 -17

2 CORINTHIANS
5:1-2
5:8
5:17
12:2

GALATIANS
5:19-21
5:22-23
6:7

EPHESIANS
1:3
4:6
6:12

PHILLIPIANS
4:13

I THESSALONIANS
1:5

2 TIMOTHY
3:16

HEBREW
1:14

I PETER
2:24

11 PETER
3: 9

REVELATIONS
21: 21

ABOUT ELDER
DR. JOSEPH LATHAN

Born in the surrounding area of Detroit Michigan and now a 18 year resident of Brooklyn, New York, Elder Dr. Joseph Lathan is the Co- Pastor of the Spiritual Israel Church & Its Army, Manhattan location. His educational background entails a Bachelor of Science degree in Psychology from Empire State College, a Master's degree in Education Administration from Michigan State University and a PhD Graduate in Organizational Leadership from the Chicago School of Professional Psychology.

Dr. Lathan's professional background includes **25+ years** in Human Services, *16 years* of service as an Ordained Minister and more than *15 years* of work experience in Education Administration at the post-secondary collegiate level.

As the youngest of 9 children born to James and Ruthie Lathan, he is happily married to Pamela Lathan for over 14 years and the father of three daughters; Erin, Paige and Jade. Additionally he has been blessed with three special grandchildren; Juliana, Allanah and the newest addition to the family, Caliana who was just recently born.

Dr. Lathan's passions include public speaking, music, singing, playing piano and spreading infectious optimism. Dr. Lathan's life philosophy and belief is that we can experience either Heaven or Hell on Earth so choose wisely.

To Learn More:

Visit his website: http://www.josephlathan.com/

PUBLICATIONS

As an expert in the field of Workplace Spirituality/Workplace Chaplaincy, Dr. Lathan's first published work, *A Narrative Study of Spirituality in the Workplace in North America*, explores the history and practice of workplace chaplaincy in the United States.

The study was conducted in the Wisconsin area with Capital Chaplains chaplaincy agency and businesses who utilize onsite workplace chaplains. Although workplace chaplaincy has been around in the U.S. for more than 30 years, the concept of having chaplains in the workplace to service the spiritual and emotional needs of employers is rather new. Companies who have or currently use onsite workplace chaplains include: Tyson Foods, Pizza Hut/Taco-Bell, Coca-Cola, and many other companies in the United States.

To order a copy on Pro Quest:
1). Visit - http://dissexpress.umi.com/dxweb/search.html
2). Search for Dissertation by:
Author: Joseph Lathan
Title: Workplace Chaplaincy: A Narrative Study of Spirituality in the Workplace in North America
ID Publication Number: 10000337
3). *To Purchase* you will have to create an account if you don't already have a Pro Quest Account

WORKPLACE
CHAPLAIN SERVICES, LLC

M any are aware of chaplains in hospitals, the military, pris-
ons and schools, but workplace chaplains are an untapped
area of care offered by Workplace Chaplain Services, LLC. From
the completion of his doctorial study, Dr. Lathan and his wife
Pamela, founded a new cutting-edge business named Workplace
Chaplain Services, LLC. Since employees spend so much of their
time in the workplace, the nature of the business is to provide help
and hope through spiritual care to workforce employees outside of
the church walls.

Chaplain Assistance Programs (CAP) is purposed to care for
employee's mind, body and spirit. Like EAP (Employee Assistance
Programs), the services are voluntary. Not only do CAP provide
the services of a EAP referral system *In-Person,* but this human
resource management tool provides a clerical element to employees who need assistance with weddings, funerals, christenings,
prayer & bible study (by request only) or provide spiritual guidance to employees who have no church home or affiliation. As
workers continue to face the uncertainties of today's workforce
(mergers, layoffs, workplace violence & workplace shootings),
Chaplain Assistance programs (CAP) are benefits that employers

offer to show genuine human- care to employees outside of hourly wages. CAP is not about proselytization or conversion but rather Productivity!!!!

Please visit the company's website at http://wpcs.us/ to learn more about this new innovative business that will one day become a vital part of companies who desire total care for their employees. The business focus is providing help and hope to employees in the workplace so that employers can focus on managing the day-to-day operation of the business.

MOTIVATIONAL SPEAKER

I f you are looking for a dynamic and inspirational motivational speaker for your upcoming workshop, luncheon, retreat or any other live event, then Dr. Lathan is a great choice. Dr. Lathan's motivational style uses personal experiences combined with biblical and spiritual principles to inspire others to overcome any barrier or challenge. Areas of expertise include, Dealing With the Loss of Love Ones, Overcoming Fear, Finding Purpose, and a plethora of topics involving Spirituality Growth and Development. Please visit the website http://www.josephlathan.com/ or email josephlathan@gmail.com to learn how to book him for your next event.